Heaven's Child

*a mother's story of tragedy
and the enduring strength of family*

Caroline Flohr

BOOK PUBLISHERS NETWORK

Book Publishers Network
P.O. Box 2256
Bothell • WA • 98041
Ph • 425-483-3040
www.bookpublishersnetwork.com

10 9 8 7 6 5 4 3 2 1

Printed in the United States of America

LCCN   2012908158
ISBN   978-1-937454-36-4

Editor: Charlotte Cook
Cover Designer: Laura Zugzda
Typographer: Stephanie Martindale
Author photograph by: Mary Grace Long

This work is a memoir based on the personal recollections and perceptions of the author. All dialogue is reconstructed from memory. Some names have been changed or omitted.

www.HeavensChild.com

In memory of my daughter, Sarah.

In honor of my children who live:
Caiti, Christopher, Mary, and Annie.

And, in thanksgiving for my husband, Andy.

Culli and Sarah, Lopez Island, age 3

contents

acknowledgements

To my family—Andy, Caiti, Christopher, Mary, Annie, Geordie, Jeff, Ginger, Ed, Orvie, and Lindy. Their support, courage, compassion, and kindness have strengthened the love we share in ways I never dreamed possible.

To Father Quigg for his faith and humor.

To Kathy Schramke, my earliest reader. Her generous encouragement, insight, and open ears moved me forward, capturing the honesty in what I was struggling to share.

To Janelle for always being there for Mary and Annie, and us.

To Nancy Rekow for asking the questions that needed asking and challenging my voice. To the members of her writing group—in particular, Bob McAllister, Everett Thompson, and Jan Cohen—for reading, suggestions, and supporting the project.

And to Charlotte Cook who, with grace and sensitivity and boundless energy, made the leap of faith to believe in my story and pull it all together!

Endless thanks to each of you—

May the road rise to meet you.
May the wind be always at your back.
May the sun shine warm upon your face.

—Irish Blessing

sarah's family

Annie	youngest sister
Mary	younger sister
Christopher	brother
Caiti	twin sister (short for Caitlin)
Caroline	mother
Andy	stepfather
Chris	father
Nonny	maternal grandmother
Papa Ed	maternal grandfather
Geordie	uncle
Jeff	uncle
Grandma, Anita	paternal grandmother
Great-grandmom, Orvie	great-grandmother
Great-granddad, Duke	great-grandfather
Mimi	great-grandmother
Papa	great-grandfather

Bainbridge Island, Washington

prologue

Tell me, what else should I have done?
Doesn't everything die at last, and too soon?
Tell me, what is it you plan to do
with your one wild and precious life?

—Mary Oliver

*B*ainbridge Island, Washington. Slightly larger than Manhattan, with canopies of evergreens and stretches of open farmland soaking up the summer sun, Bainbridge is a special place. The island is five miles wide and ten miles long, with a rural feel, but only a thirty-five-minute ferry ride to downtown Seattle.

The main street through town—Winslow Way—has restaurants, bakeries, and boutiques. In a culture where few people know their neighbors, here there is a sense of community. At the Saturday Farmer's Market, neighbors meet and greet. Crime is significantly lower than the national average. People still leave their doors unlocked and their keys in the car.

Unlike most American families, at least one parent usually stays home with the kids while the other makes the weekday commute into Seattle. In some families—those lucky enough to telecommute or have their own home business—both parents are around. The schools have a lot of parental support, and volunteerism is the norm. The public high school sends 97 percent of its graduates to college.

Summer on Bainbridge is mild and sunny, with long, lazy days. After the damp, gray winters, our days are shaped around warm-weather pastimes. We wonder why anyone would leave the island in summer to vacation elsewhere, saving our travel for the winter when darkness sets in before 5:00 p.m. and chilly rain cuts to the bone.

Many of the beaches on Bainbridge Island are private, but many streets dead-end at public beaches, some hidden. These areas attract the local teens—bonfires on summer nights, a place to launch kayaks, little Eden's with no parents. When two or three gather, dozens follow.

Over half the population of twenty-three thousand is under the age of eighteen. And like kids everywhere, they complain of boredom, fantasizing about life in California or Hawaii or some remote worldly destination. Teenagers from elsewhere would rather be on Bainbridge.

When I migrated from Seattle with my children in tow, Bainbridge Island seemed an idyllic place for them to grow up. But, as I would learn, even idyllic places have their perils.

the years before bainbridge

*In every conceivable manner,
the family is link to our past,
bridge to our future.*

—Alexis Haley

Caiti and Sarah were my first pregnancy and my first children. During the first four months, nausea followed me everywhere, all day long. After it finally passed, I started eating enough for five people. The fantasy about the glow of motherhood left me wan, discouraged, and ashen.

An early pregnancy test solved the mystery. Not one baby, but two—each distinct and intact—each facing the other, as if looking in a mirror.

I wasn't sure how to handle one baby, no less two. I grew up in a neighborhood full of boys, never played with dolls. At fourteen, I went away to boarding school. At twenty-four, I had never even held a baby.

But nature took over, and for thirty-eight weeks, twin A, twin B, and I prepared for a life together, three hearts beating in unison. The twins were born February 5, 1988.

Caiti was the first to arrive, Sarah two hours later. They were "mirror-image twins." Caiti was right-handed, Sarah, left-handed. Caiti's hair parted on the right, Sarah's, on the left. Caiti's first cavity was the back right tooth, Sarah's, the back left tooth. Caiti avoided risk; Sarah thrived on the edge. For as long as they were together, each was half of a whole.

Growing up, they shared the same bedroom, even shared the same crib for the first eight months. They went to bed and woke up at the same time. They shared the same bathroom, ate the same favorite foods—macaroni and cheese, plain peanut butter sandwiches, and cheese pizza. Over and over, they watched *Cinderella*. They shared the same classrooms and teachers, the same friends, played on the same teams. Each February, they had a combined birthday party, where the presents were "theirs." Hardly ever was anything "mine." Every hour of every day, Caiti and Sarah functioned as a unit, not as individuals. They were referred to as "The Twins"—only occasionally by their given names. Rarely did we speak to them, or about them, separately and individually. And, rarely did I spend individual time with Caiti or Sarah. Life moved along for them as was expected, always together.

When Chris and I married, he was a musician with dreams of becoming a rock star—a songwriter with a charismatic stage presence. We began married life in New York City, but less than a year later when a cab cut us off crossing Central Park, we moved to Seattle, my hometown. We supported ourselves with odd jobs. A few months after the move, I found myself pregnant with twins. The next day, Chris began applying to law schools.

Seven months later, he entered law school at the University of Puget Sound in Tacoma. But with an hour commute each way, along with evening study sessions and summer internships, he was rarely home. Most of the time, the babies and I were alone.

My body couldn't handle breastfeeding one baby, let alone two, so we needed formula and twice as much of everything. Disposables were expensive so I used cloth diapers. There were no movie dates, no babysitters, no extras. Our monthly budget was stretched to the limit.

Caiti and Sarah, 8 months old

At the top of Queen Anne Hill, overlooking downtown Seattle and the Space Needle, our third-floor walkup was sadly in need of repairs. Every day, up and down three flights of stairs, I hauled baskets of clothes down to the basement, carried groceries up, and took trash out, navigating with one twin in a sling on my chest, the other in a backpack.

To pass the long days, we rode the Seattle Metro buses, strolled the sidewalks, and picnicked in the parks. I learned to plumb the kitchen sink and cook the Thanksgiving turkey. I sewed. We were frugal, but we were fine.

Caiti and Sarah didn't speak to anyone except each other until they were three and a half years old, living in a world of their own with its own language—a strange babble of song-like vowels—with me as their only interpreter.

grandmom

Beginning in the fall of 1989, twice a week, for fourteen months, Grandmom babysat Caiti and Sarah, now nineteen months old, while I finished my engineering degree at the University of Washington.

She was seventy-one years old and had raised five children. Her friends called her Orvie. Pink cheeks with wispy white clouds of hair, she always welcomed us with a smile, wiping her wet hands on a freshly laundered apron around her waist and reaching out with a big hug. Despite her age, she exuded youth. Even the wrinkled skin on her hands was softer than mine. She wore rubber gloves to wash the dishes and leather gloves when leaving the house. A jar of Pond's Cold Cream was a fixture on the windowsill above the kitchen sink. The twins loved her.

Caiti and Sarah, age 4

Grandmom was calm and spiritual, gracious and understanding. Details mattered. She ironed creases into her pants and starched her Peter Pan collars. Her days had continuity and routine. Every morning she prayed the rosary, enjoyed a cup of weak, black coffee with a breakfast of sourdough toast and whatever melon was in season, and attended Mass.

As the twins got older, we'd sit on her kitchen floor and watch her cook, then move into the TV room for dinner. When the twins asked her questions, she gave straightforward, conclusive answers that would invariably lead to other questions, which led to more conversation. She spoke to adults, grandchildren, and great-grandchildren with the same clarity and respect. And we all understood.

Years later, when she was a preteen, Sarah asked Grandmom, "Do you believe in ghosts?" After telling a short tale of how her Great-aunt Josephine appeared at the foot of her bed, Grandmom answered simply, "I believe."

But, she didn't just believe; she knew for certain there was something beyond this life. Her confidence and comfort drew you into her conviction that we would all journey on after we died. I watched as the twins absorbed her stories, mulling over questions to ask. I wondered if Sarah's interpretation of a ghost was the same as Grandmom's.

Duke, Carol, Ginger (in rocking chair), Orvie, Lindy, 1940s

sarah

Sarah named herself "FlowerBlack" in August 1991, when she was three. I was sewing holiday dresses for the twins with fabric snagged from the remnant table at Hancock Fabrics, only two dollars per yard. Black velvet for the bodice and sleeves, dark green plaid tartan for the skirt and sash.

Sarah grabbed some scraps from under my old sewing table that sat near an attic window at the end of a narrow walk-through closet. She sat on the floor beside me rubbing her flush cheeks with the velvet pieces, calmed by the silky smoothness of the fabric. After a while, she found a long rectangular scrap, about a foot wide, with an almost perfect cut line and no frayed edges. She settled back, draped it over her head and jammed a black hairband over the velvet to hold it in. "I'm FlowerBlack," she said.

After that she wore the fabric scrap everywhere, from waking to bedtime, until just past her fourth birthday. It became her signature. She demanded that everyone call her "FlowerBlack," except for Caiti, her twin.

I guess Sarah was just tired of being called one of "The Twins." She thought the new name suited her, made her more herself. Who knows why she thought of herself as a flower?

One late fall afternoon 1991, while Sarah was still in her "FlowerBlack" stage, I parked Mimi's (my paternal grandmother who died when I was almost twenty-one) old blue Ford Thunderbird—on loan from my Papa; long and low to the ground like a Lincoln Continental with two heavy doors, a V-8 engine that purred, dark blue velvet seats saturated with cigarette smoke—and walked my twins down Broadway to rent a movie at Blockbuster Video. If you wanted to be unique in Seattle, Broadway, reeking of Goth fashion, was the place to hang. Sarah, wearing her velvet headpiece, was dressed all in black that day. She didn't always wear black. Sometimes it was pink or purple or orange floral with her black velvet head wrap. Strolling along to the video store, not one person took a second glance. My child fit right in with the counterculture.

At first, I tried to persuade Sarah to discard the FlowerBlack look whenever we left the house. But she refused, staring me down, eyes squinted like a cat ready to pounce, hands pressed against her hips, legs squared and knees locked. I let it pass.

papa

Even her great-grandfather, whom we all called Papa, never said a word about the hairpiece. Dressed in his uniform—dark suit, tie, and white shirt—he smiled at this child as if she'd been born with a black velvet head of hair. Papa understood the value of choosing your battles.

Eighty years old when Caiti and Sarah were born, Papa was a survivor of the Great Depression. He believed in the power of education, worked hard, and contributed to his community. America was his country, Seattle his hometown, and the Pacific Northwest was "God's Country." Although a world traveler, Papa stated in no uncertain terms that the San Juan Islands were as beautiful as any place on earth.

Our strict budget was his idea for those law school years. But, he made sure we didn't do without. Some days he would leave a quart of strawberries or two steaks on the back stoop of our walkup. Sometimes, he would stay and visit. The twins were the first babies he'd ever held. Until now, he'd spent much of his life at the office.

When the twins were two, Papa found a house just a five-minute walk from his and helped us with the down payment. What a luxury to have our own washer and dryer and dishwasher and enough hot water to fill the tub. No more climbing three flights of stairs.

He loved showing off the twins to his friends in the neighborhood. Some days, the four of us stopped to feed the ducks. Some days, we had cookies at Madison Park Bakery. Most summer days were spent at the family cabin—Geordie, my oldest brother, lived there year-round-- on Lopez Island, playing on the beach, building forts out of driftwood, or digging clams for eating later. When I was a child, Mimi made a wicked New England clam chowder.

Papa and the twins,
digging clams at the cabin on Lopez Island

Two days after the twins' fourth birthday, Papa had a sudden heart attack. Not understanding the seriousness of his condition, I left Caiti home with her dad, and drove to the hospital with Sarah, one of the few times the twins spent apart. Had I chosen clearly and left Sarah home, a birthday celebration would've been her last memory of him.

Instead, we entered a room of impending death. Papa was deathly pale. Machines were churning. Tubes ran every direction, in and out of his body. There was a strange odor.

Two days later, Papa died, and that night, with no explanation, Sarah took off her black velvet head wrap and threw it away. I rescued it from the garbage and have it still.

christopher

In September 1993, Christopher was born, an event of little importance to the twins. After two babies the first time out, having a single was a walk in the park. An easy child with a calm temperament, Christopher slept all night, ate well, and progressed smoothly through early childhood. As soon as he could hold his helmeted head upright in the bike carrier, we rode for miles each day. He was a delightful companion, my new best friend.

Christopher, age 4

The extended family expanded when my mother and stepfather moved back to Seattle just before Christopher was born. After my parents' divorce when I was ten, we moved to Bakersfield, California. Like most kids, I was confused and frightened when my dad left. I remembered him leaving the house but couldn't recall anyone explaining why, or if he would return. He didn't. I've seen him very few times since then.

My dad and my brothers, Lopez Island, summer 1973

Almost five years later in August 1998, two weeks after Princess Diana's tragic accident, I filed for divorce. I remember watching TV, every station tuned to news of Diana's accident, the kids sacked out on floor pillows, eyes glued to the screen. The twins were ten, Christopher almost five.

Spring 1999, the kids and I moved to Bainbridge Island. A short time later, their dad moved to Montana.

the firehouse

Our new home was an old firehouse, declined for traditional financing because the appraiser marked it "uninhabitable." It wasn't much, but I had never been happier.

The Firehouse, May 1999

For me, the divorce felt like shedding an overloaded backpack that had burned ruts in my shoulders. But, the twins took it very hard. They raged against me and raged against their dad, as if the two of them were pitted against the world. With strength in their solidarity, I was now the outsider.

Christopher was my mainstay. When we moved to Bainbridge, he was five. By age six, he was competent with power tools, preparing our shower stall for tile, handling simple cuts on a miter saw, and mowing the lawn. Together, we remodeled an outbuilding on our property, nailed shingles to the roof, insulated the walls, ditched the utility lines, and buffed it out, ready-to-rent. We made a good team.

Summers, the twins' outbursts mellowed a bit. Collecting juicy blackberries from brambles lining the roads, they would arrive home with purple hands and crush the buckets of berries with an old rubber mallet. Together, we dumped the fruit into a big pot on the stove, turned up the flame, stirred in too many cups of white sugar, and as the mixture thickened, added the pectin. The summer breeze pushed the heat through the kitchen and out the opposite row of windows. For days or weeks after the canning party, the girls would set up a small wooden table at the corner of Fort Ward Hill Road and Parkview and sell their jam. Sarah saved every dollar she earned.

First summer on Bainbridge Island, 1999

andy arrives

About three years later, I reconnected with an old friend. Andy and I had met at summer camp when we were children. He was skinny then, with short dark hair that grew shaggier as he got older. At ten, our legs were the same length and width, our ankles and calves the same size, but he could sure outrun me. During that summer at camp, we shared a first kiss, and he became my boyfriend for three summers. At twenty, we lost touch, though he remained friends with my brother, Geordie.

At thirty-six when we met again, I was living alone at the firehouse with my kids.

Andy's life had been very different from mine. He had climbed almost every fourteener in Colorado—almost all fifty-three peaks—plus Mt. McKinley and Mt. Aconcagua, the highest peaks in the Americas. On powder days, he was on the slopes for "first tracks," skiing every double black diamond with the grace of a soaring eagle. With each full moon, he rock-climbed—unharnessed—the faces of the Rocky Mountains and traveled the globe in search of the greatest fly-fishing rivers and best surfing spots. In his twenties, buried by an avalanche a quarter-mile wide and fifty-feet high, he punched a hole in the ice for air and clawed his way to the surface. Another man perished.

the second marriage

In 2002, Andy and I were married. At the same time, my ex-husband, now living in Montana, married a woman with a son a year younger than Christopher.

Andy and Christopher bonded right away. But, the twins continued with their rage and dismay. Andy had no children of his own and suddenly found himself in a war zone. Sarah had shown her fierce temper early on; now it was totally out of control. Her unrelenting rage was frightening to Andy. The screaming and name-calling was unbearable to me. And, I was pregnant.

taking leave

By the beginning of the twins' freshman year of high school, we had moved from skirmishes to battles to a full-blown war. Caiti and Sarah often refused to follow house rules, including curfew. There were threats and accusations and more name-calling. The police had been called out more than once.

With a new marriage, Christopher upset and confused by the chaos, and a five-month pregnancy, I finally lost my stamina and resolve. The only possibility I could see was to take a breather and send the twins to live with their dad for a while.

I put in a call to my mother. That same day, my stepfather came to Bainbridge, collected the twins, and put them on the next plane to Montana. That day was the lowest moment in my life.

What I hoped would be a cooling-off period was a bitter failure. Their stepmother had no interest in dealing with the angst and anger of belligerent teenage girls and resented the sudden intrusion into their small home, which now had to accommodate a family of five. But most unfortunate was the chasm between their dad and me that prevented us from working together to find a better solution.

It was decided that Caiti would remain in Montana and Sarah would be dispatched to New York City to live with her grandma, Anita Gillette, an accomplished Broadway actress, who extended unconditional love and opened her home without reservations.

Anita dancing with Sarah

When Caiti was asked about the separation from Sarah during that time, she said, "All we wanted was to be with our mom. We knew we had each other, but we thought we had lost her forever." Just before Christmas 2002, Sarah returned to Seattle to live with my brother, Jeff, and Caiti came home to Bainbridge. It had been the most time the twins had ever been apart.

The bitterness between Sarah and Andy would take time to heal, and no one was willing to risk more of the gut-wrenching upheaval. I was nine months pregnant with Mary when I arrived alone to furnish and decorate Sarah's upstairs bedroom at Jeff's house.

She entered an all-girls' Catholic school in Bellevue. Caiti returned to Bainbridge High. Andy and I welcomed our daughter, Mary, that January, in 2003. When school was out, Sarah came home. Between my mother, Jeff, and Geordie, she had been well cared for, and I was extremely grateful. I felt complete having Sarah home, four children under one roof again, and I was pregnant with my fifth.

Tensions resurfaced as the summer progressed, and it was decided that Sarah would return to school in Bellevue. It took just four days to realize that the two-hour commute each way wasn't feasible. We had to work it out at home.

In early November 2003, we took a family trip to Hawaii. Whether change washed in with the warm waters of Waikiki or, perhaps, because the twins were seeing home in a different light, Sarah's rages and unruliness subsided. Pleasant, engaged, respectful, and fun, we liked each other again. Most of the time, she and Andy were not at each other's throats. I wasn't asking for perfect. I was asking for better.

Caiti and Sarah, Waikiki, November 2003

time runs out

By the summer of 2004, we had a second baby, Annie, making us a family of seven. Caring for my family filled my days and interrupted my sleep. Caiti and Sarah were sixteen years older than my youngest child, Annie. With Mary just a year older than Annie, life was a blur of activity.

That summer, an outbreak of acne made Sarah a little self-conscious. She hung out at home with me, took pottery classes, and studied German at the language school in downtown Seattle. In late July, we took a family trip to Whistler.

Sarah, Papa Ed, Nonny, and Caiti, July 2004

In mid-August, Caiti was admitted to Children's Medical Center in Seattle for an anxiety disorder. Each morning, for ten days, Sarah and I rode the ferry to visit Caiti. Those ten days were the most time Sarah and I had ever shared alone. How could I have known it was our last chance?

 *august* 2004

You must do the thing you think you cannot do.
—Eleanor Roosevelt

Monday, August 23, 5:30 a.m., I awake to sharp knocking at the front door. Was I was dreaming? Sarah's voice runs through my head. *"Don't be afraid. I promise I won't leave you."*

More knocks, louder this time. I pull my stiff body from the twin bed in Annie's room after another long night of her sleeplessness. Andy must be in our bedroom after returning late from Utah and getting Christopher on his flight to Montana. A single ray of sunshine filters through the trees, crosses the maple floors, and rebounds off the yellow walls.

Peering over the balcony from the top of the stairs, an old blue cotton robe flung over my shoulders—more knocks—I'm not alarmed, just curious. It's very early. Emmett, our fat old chocolate lab, refuses to stir.

I've had more than my share of interrupted nights—drunk teenagers, broken curfews, cell phones not answered. I know the drill. "This is Officer So 'n' So. Sarah's at a party at such and such address. You need to come pick her up." I'm annoyed.

Opening the front door, I'm facing two middle-aged men, official-looking and disheveled. One wears a dirty firefighter's uniform, dirty hands, black boots scuffed and muddy. The second man, shorter and stockier, wears dark pants and a short black jacket zipped over his white shirt. He wears dark walking shoes and his hands are clean. Both look exhausted. Anxiety begins to creep up the back of my neck.

The firefighter moves closer, his face covered with black smudges and a few bloody scratches. "Are you Sarah's mother, Caroline?"

My hands begin to shake. I can't answer. Fear is rooting my bare feet to the floor. Quietly and carefully, I ask, "Would you like to come in? Should I wake my husband?"

"Thank you. Yes." His dark eyes are blank. I feel unsteady climbing the stairs. Shaking Andy gently, I say, "Two men are here. Please get up."

In the living room, we sit next to each other on the velvet green sofa. Emmett sits upright at my feet. Our bodies do not touch.

The firefighter clears his throat. "There's been an accident, and Sarah has been killed."

I don't understand right away. I cock my head to the side as though someone has struck me, as though I'm not able to register the words. My breathing goes shallow. I don't want to hear this or think it or know it. It is too enormous to bear. And then, with a stunning blow of recognition, I wonder if I have lost them both.

Barely above a whisper, I ask the firefighter, "Was Caiti in the accident? They're twins."

"No," the man answers, squaring his eyes with mine.

I jump to my feet and dash down the stairs. I have to see for myself. How does he know the dead girl is Sarah? How does he know Caiti isn't with her? How does he know Sarah has a twin sister?

Sweating, heart pounding, body shaking, I crack open the door, and peer in. The white chenille bedspread lifts with the rhythm of Caiti's heart. I feel it beat with mine.

Pulling myself back up the stairs, I sit down next to Andy. Not a word passes between us. Emmett lays his large head on my lap and raises his curious eyes to meet mine. Everything is in slow motion.

The man in the short black coat says, "The coroner will be contacting you this morning. Here's my card, if I can be of any assistance. I'm sorry."

They let themselves out. No details are requested. None are given. How can I know, for sure, that the news delivered by two strangers is true, that my child is dead? Do they have the right house?

A dreadful quiet fills the room. My thoughts begin to race. It isn't Sarah. They've made a mistake. Finally, the throbbing in my ears becomes thunderous, and the truth washes over me. Sarah is gone.

The tears begin that moment. I couldn't know then that they would flow for the next five years, every day, and every night.

I don't know how much time passes. When I am able to stand, I struggle downstairs to Caiti's bedroom, the second time that morning. I turn the cold doorknob and hesitate. A tangle of clothes litters the carpet. How peaceful she looks—her face creamy—a mirror image of Sarah. She is breathing gently, like my youngest children.

I sit on the edge of her bed, wrapping her left hand in both of mine. Her eyes flutter open and she looks into my eyes. There are no words. She begins to wail and scream and rip at her hair, her grief and terror filling the room and breaking through the walls.

It could have been a day or an hour or a minute, but after floods of tears have been spent and her agony has quieted, I take her in my arms, and we sit there holding each other for a long time. Later, I half-carry her up the stairs to the living room, settle her on the sofa, and tuck her into Granddad's mohair blanket.

The three of us collect in that space—I, on the edge of Granddad's brown chair; Caiti, small, fragile, distant; Andy, sitting silently, unmoving. Our youngest girls asleep upstairs. I desperately wish for Christopher to be home, frantically regretting that he caught that light-night flight to Montana after flying home with Andy from bike races in Utah.

Finally, Caiti is calm enough to hear me. "Sarah's been in an accident. I don't know what happened. She's dead." I say it twice.

Caiti struggles to find words, "Who was she with? Where was she? I talked to her at 11:30. She was in bed ..." Andy puts a hand on her shoulder. "I'll make some coffee," he says.

No more words. I have never known such silence. And, even in that moment, devastated by grief, I fully realize how grateful I am that Caiti was not in that car. I am grateful that my other children are safe.

At 6:30 a.m., I feel strong enough to call my mother. But when she answers, the sobs break through, "Accident ... Sarah killed ... waiting for the coroner's call ... don't know ... don't know...don't know."

"We'll be on the next boat," she says and hangs up. The coffee is ready.

Fumbling through a kitchen drawer, I pull out my address book to call Sarah's dad. The phone rings again and again and again before he answers.

"Chris, this is Caroline. There's been an accident. Sarah was killed." He wants details. "I don't know," I tell him. "The coroner hasn't called." His voice quakes, and then bursts into a wail like an animal, horribly wounded and terrified. We've become strangers since the divorce. I don't know what more to say.

Though he still sees Christopher a few times a year, his time with the twins has dwindled, and now, dissolved. Our children have suffered so much from our anger and resentment. Guilt gnaws around the edges of my nerves. I am afraid they can never forgive us. I promise to call back when I have more information.

Thankfully, Mary and Annie are still asleep, soft breathing filtering through the baby monitor. I've brought them into this world to know love, life, and laughter—not tears, sadness, and confusion. Now death hovers over us. When my parents arrive, Mother moves upstairs to be with them.

the coroner

Finally, at 10:30 a.m., the call comes.

"This is Harvey Clapp, the county coroner. I'm sorry about Sarah. Emergency personnel at the scene knew her. She has a small fighting Irishman tattooed over her left hip, to the left of her bellybutton. Is that correct?"

Breathing into my anxiety, I whisper, "Yes, that's correct." It is Sarah, after all. My Sarah.

Mr. Clapp continues, "We'll do an autopsy. You can have the funeral home call me." He tells me to expect the death certificate in about a month and the toxicology report in about six weeks. "Any questions?"

"No. Thank you for your help," I stammer.

"I'm sorry," he says again. He never asks me to identify Sarah, never asks if I want to see her one last time. I don't think I could bear to see my daughter's dead body. He gives no details of the accident, and I ask for none. In that moment, asphyxiated by grief, I don't need to know more.

We pay so little attention to daily life. Ask people what they were doing on any given Wednesday a month or so ago, and they'll say they have no idea. But today, I want to remember everything. When did I last see Sarah? What were we doing? What did we say? Around 4:00 p.m. yesterday, she waved goodbye and said, "I love you, Mama." Only yesterday.

She was carrying a box of Macaroni & Cheese she'd taken from the freezer, shoving the cell phone into her back pocket. Caiti drove her to a friend's house to spend the night. If I had known I was seeing her sapphire eyes and her generous smile for the last time ...

Who pulled her limp body from the car? Did she die right away? Who recognized her by the fighting Irishman tattoo? Who closed the lids over her vacant eyes and draped a white sheet over her body? Who was involved in the accident? When was she killed? Where was she killed? How did all this happen? What *had* she been thinking?

All the questions I hadn't been able to ask are racing through my mind.

There is no manual to consult when your child dies; no step-by-step guide in the how-to books on the library shelves. We can only do our best, and that has to be good enough.

Chris picks up right away when I call back. We are calm and congenial in deciding how best to take care of our daughter. For a moment, I wonder why it takes a tragedy to leave the past behind and put our children first. There are no arguments. Chris will fly to Seattle. I will make the funeral arrangements.

Andy calls my brother, Jeff, who calls our family priest, one of Sarah's favored people. For three generations, Father Quigg has been our spiritual guide: baptisms, communions, confirmations, marriages, annulments, last rites for the old—and now a burial for the young. On Christmas Eve, he offers our traditional Mass at Jeff's house. Right along with the children, he competes every Easter for the golden egg. For meals and good stories, he's a regular. He finds humor in Sarah's fighting Irishman tattoo (which I don't find humorous at all) while promising to marry her off to a nice Irish boy.

Jeff also phones the cemetery. Our family plot has rested at Calvary, Seattle's Catholic cemetery, near the University of Washington since the late 1800s, beginning with the burial of my great-great-uncle George L'Abbe Jr., who died of cancer at the age of five. The last death in our family was my Papa's, twelve years before. There is a plot available below Papa's and Mimi's, below the row of six family graves. This will be Sarah's place.

I've never needed to discuss burial plots or consider the choice of a casket or an urn, burial versus cremation, burial versus scattering the ashes. But since the Church is now open to cremation, cremation will be my choice. A private service is scheduled for Thursday, August 26, 2004, at 11 a.m., three days after the accident.

The painful reality is setting in. Sarah will never dance at the senior prom or graduate in cap and gown. She'll never show off her fighting Irishman tattoo at Notre Dame or celebrate her twenty-first birthday. Never a first love. Never a wedding. Never a child of her own.

My mother calls her mother, Sarah's great-grandmother, who then calls her other children—two in Seattle and two in California—who then call my eight cousins. Sarah has died.

Caiti and I move slowly up the stairs to the master bathroom with Emmett close behind. The sound of hot, running water drowns out the voices in the kitchen below. I gather up a washcloth, clean towel, new razor and toothbrush, and a bottle of shower gel, rubbing her shoulders as the tub fills. Both of us stare out the window to the forest beyond. The water gives way as she settles into the hot bath and folds into a fetal position.

When she is dry and warm, I tuck her into my bed, only to discover a while later that she has moved into Sarah's room, clenching the remains of Sarah's tattered baby blanket, her wet hair matted on the pillow. It is to become a familiar sight.

By Monday morning, Caiti has disappeared into her own world. While I move about, numb and in shock but fully aware of my reality, she sleeps and dreams. Awake, her eyes are vacant. She has lost the other half of herself.

Thirteen hours after the accident, details begin to trickle in. A Bainbridge police officer comes to the house with more details—names of the passengers and the injuries sustained. I listen closely as if searching for Sarah's voice in the wreckage. Eight teens in an SUV ... Sarah in a friend's lap in the back jumper seat ... her friend airlifted to the trauma center ... his name, Connor, the only familiar name.

More and more questions race through my mind. Those last moments of her life must have been filled with terror. Did she suffer for seconds? Minutes? Did she feel the air vibrate with the shrill screams of kids still alive in the car? Did she feel the grinding of a saw blade, metal against metal, as the car was torn apart? Did she feel her body being tugged from the seat? Was she wearing a seat belt? Hardest of all ... why, out of eight teenagers, is my daughter the only one who died?

Word is spreading fast on the island. A friend of Caiti's, who lives near the scene of the accident arrives to lend support. Eyes wide, voice gentle, he says, "I just passed a tow truck coming here. That car was flat as a pancake." His fresh face shows disbelief, as if he is amazed that anyone could have survived.

People reach out to us. People who love us. People who don't know us. People who never liked us. By Monday afternoon, flowers start to arrive. I'll always remember the first delivery—a potted blue hydrangea, atop a square green stepping stone.

Baskets and baskets follow. Simple bouquets, vases of cut flowers, elaborate mixed arrangements. Live plants and trees for the yard. Even rosebushes with angelic names. Enough to fill a whole garden.

Each message assures us that Sarah will not be forgotten. Each message absorbs an ounce of our pain. Each message tells us we are not alone in our grief. I stage the front steps by size, color, pot, and texture, as if decorating our house. I bring in a simple vase of pink Gerbera daisies to set on the kitchen windowsill. Pink is Caiti's favorite color. Sarah's, blue.

Nonny and Caiti

For my mother, caring for her children has always come first. Though we are both petite women, her presence fills the room. Bobbed salt-and-pepper hair clipped straight across her neck, square jawline, and well-defined cheekbones, my mother walks with intention—shoulders flung back, posture erect. The pink tint of her skin softens her face. Her children look like her. My children look like me. Same features, same mannerisms. My mother speaks calmly, processing each word. I've never heard her curse. If there has been a constant in my life since my divorce, it is she—safe, secure, comforting, clear.

By late afternoon, she scoops up Mary and Annie and takes them home with her. Bundled in blankets and laid to sleep on a comforter beside her bed, the girls sleep through the night for the first time in their short lives.

No one told me that grief felt so like fear.
—C. S. Lewis

Late Monday night, twenty hours after the accident, Andy is asleep in our bedroom while I sit quietly in Sarah's room. An odd clarity directs me as I rummage through boxes of mementoes, trophies and medals, school photos, old stuffed animals, the pottery she has formed with her hands. I look through her art portfolio and read her poetry, finding one of my favorite pieces, written when she was eleven:

Life is but a Test

Life is but a test to see what we can do,
to see what we can give.
Life is what we do,
Love is what we give.

Suddenly, there it is; the scrap of black velvet she'd found under my sewing table thirteen years ago during her FlowerBlack period.

I hold her hairbrush and pull a strand of molasses-colored hair, then arrange the collection of perfume bottles in a perfect row. I gaze out at the calla lilies, now furled, and hold her burgundy shirt to my heart, breathing in her soft smell, imagining that she stands beside me. It is Tuesday, August 24, at 2:20 a.m. Will the sun ever break through this dark night?

Opening the top drawer of her desk, I find Sarah's red wallet. Why didn't she have it with her? Here is her ASB card from school, her driver's permit, her debit card, and several dollars. Her permit shows the small red heart indicating that she is an organ donor. Pulling out the stack of papers, I find an empty vial of cheap vodka stashed in the back of the drawer. I notice an essay marked with a 50/50 and the teacher's comments. It is titled, *"The Power of One Personal Narrative."*

I've never seen this. My knees buckle, and I drop onto the lamb's wool rug beside the bed. I reach for Emmett and read aloud as if to a child.

Sarah
The Power of One Personal Narrative
May 19, 2004

Part 1: The End

It is hard to imagine that any end could ever lead to a beginning, but many times in life it does. And in my case, I must begin with the end. Like many marriages, my parent's marriage ended in divorce. I will not dwell on the deep hurt we suffered during that time, but realize, that from this pain the path of my life was born. I was ten years old when the end dawned upon the Gillette family. For the next four years, my life was essentially a world of hatred. I was a storm of anger, pain, and resentment, ignited from Le Divorce and many, many close-to-heart complications.

During this time, my mom moved away from my beloved Madison Park, and moved to Bainbridge Island. I hated her for this, and during the weeks when I had to be with her, I longed for the weekend when I was to be with my dad, in Madison Park, where the sun shined, the blossoming pink cherry trees lined the streets, and familiarity cushioned me. But, as we all must learn at some point, time changes everything. My happy days with dad were to come to an abrupt end, when a new figure entered my life. Her name was Amy. The epitome of evil, I related her to the Evil Stepmother in Cinderella. During those days when my dad and Amy still lived in Madison Park, life could tend to be on the hellish side. One night in particular, I remember having disgusting particles of food thrown on us during our sleep because, to their dismay, we had left food in the sink after doing the dishes. I suffered deep hurt from my father's harsh transformation. He had deserted us. Days turned into weeks, weeks into months, and eventually months into years; and it was not until recently that I finally accepted that my dad was *never coming back; this was the man he had become, and the man he always will be.*

Eventually, my father moved to Montana with Amy. It is always hard to accept such things as these, to acknowledge your father has a new family, and to realize that you are not part of it. But with time, I learned one of the greatest survival skills of all,; and this is the capability of going numb. It is only when you can deal with no more pain, that your mind allows you to go numb, and I have mastered it. Perhaps my hurt was due to my inability to cope with change, but great pain I endured, nonetheless, as time moved on. After Amy, I was by no means ready to accept the coming of Andy, my stepfather. I hated them both, and I wore my hate on the outside, causing trouble in my wake. Life kept going, and pain kept coming, until I found myself at the dawn of a new era. High school. However, it was not to be.

I'd rather not speak of what happened on the 3rd of September of that year, but what I can tell you, is that it was to change the rest of my life. It's weird to think that one day could be such a turning point in someone's life, but I suppose that we go through everything for a reason, and the next day I found myself on a plane for Montana.

It took my father three weeks to figure out what to do with me. During those three weeks, I lived in an army hotel with one bedroom and 4 other people. I cannot begin to tell you how deeply those three weeks affected me, and although it has been rather overlooked, I am going to make a point of it now. I had never before had to listen to anybody, yet alone my father and my stepmother, yell at each other about how they didn't want me there. I had never felt so unwanted before in my life, but by then I had become accustomed to such a feeling. The local playground soon became our hangout spot during the day as we waited for our dad to come back to the hotel room from work, and I can tell you, that those days were some of the loneliest days of my life.

When my father finally decided to send me to New York City to live with my grandma, I was just happy to get out of there. I was ready to start my new life and settle down in the Big City.

Part 2: New York

It is rather funny to hear people on Bainbridge talking about how they want to move to New York City when they grow up. They obviously have no idea what it is like to live in such a city. When I got there, I found myself living in a one- bedroom apartment sleeping in a cot next to one of the most dramatic and overwhelming women I have ever met; my grandma, the actress. I will admit that I learned a lot about life during those 4 months. However, during this time, I closed up as a person, rarely talked, and found myself slipping away into depression. This made it extremely difficult to get along with my grandma, who is a very open, talkative, and emotional person. I preferred to keep my feelings to myself, and I have realized that bottling these up may have been the cause for the anger that I harbored in my heart for the next year. I never talked to my mother, nor my father, who had both made it clear that they didn't want me. I learned in New York City how to be independent, keep to myself, and most importantly, how to go numb.

The first couple of weeks in New York City were extremely hectic as my grandmother and I tried frantically to enroll me in school. For three days, I attended a school basically for juvenile delinquents. When I realized I was in the wrong place, I transferred to a very nice private Waldorf School on 5th Avenue. I will not say that my time in New York City was horrible, because truthfully, it was not. I loved looking in the windows of the classy upper Eeastside shops. I loved walking outside in the morning to find freshly fallen snow on the world's most magnificent city, and, for the most part, I loved the hustle and bustle of the city. But most of all, I loved the crazy characters I met. New York City is definitely something else. However, at the time, I was too heartbroken to realize all I had in front of me. It is odd how one can feel so alone with millions of people around you. Towards the end of the semester, we all knew that things were not working out. My grandma and I were a genera-tion apart, and getting along with her was extremely difficult because of the personality clash. So my mother made plans for me to move in with my Uncle Jeff--—that would prove to be my next adventure.

Part 3: The Uncles

I was 14 years old when I moved to Bellevue to live with my Uncle Jeff and my Uncle Geordie. My Uncle Jeff is a suc-cessful business type of guy, while my Uncle Geordie is exactly the opposite--—a pure Hippie. My uncle Geordie lived in the basement. Jeff had decided to take him in because, just like me, he also had nowhere to go. He deals with severe alcohol problems and is very "out there;"; however, he is nonetheless just as great as Jeff is. Both my uncles have distinct personali-ties, which were both fun to experience. We all lived in a huge empty house on Clyde Hill, and we were just like roommates. Despite my age, I was given all the freedom in the world, which may not have been so good for me. Although living with my two uncles was very fun, it often had its down-points. Most of the time, Jeff was at work and had his own life to deal with, and Geordie had his own life too, so I found myself at home all the time by myself, in a big empty and lonely house. There were no meal, no parental guidance, and I did not receive the kind of love that only a parent can give a child. I often had to deal with Geordie's drunkenness, which definitely got very irritating. Many nights my crying echoed throughout the bare house when no one was home, and I still could not find the happiness that I needed.

I attended Forest Ridge of the Sacred Heart Convent, a private all-girls Catholic school. My personality began to blossom at the school because of how comfortable I felt. I made people laugh, which felt really good. But most of these laughs came from putting myself down, and inside, my self-esteem lacked.

As summer rolled around, my mother was making new plans for me. Since living with my uncles had only been temporary, she decided that I could finally come home.

Part 4: The Summer

Home. How nervous I was to live with my mother again. I would also be living with my sister, who had come home from Montana at the beginning of 2nd semester. However, when I got home, anger just grew inside me. I will keep my summer story short, because, frankly, there is not much to say. I spent the summer out and about, and things with my family were never mended. I still harbored much hate for my stepdad and much anger towards my mom, and this just led to more problems towards the end of the summer. In the end, things did not work out. School started up again, and after the first day of commuting from Bainbridge to Bellevue to go to Forest Ridge, I think my mom gave up. I was kicked out again. My bags and I were dropped off on my best friend's doorstep. I lived with Kelly for about the first 3 weeks of school, and after one week of attempting to attend Forest Ridge on the eastside, I gave up and dropped out.

Part 5: The Ghetto

Living with Kelly in her room was obviously not a permanent choice. So, the most unlikely character stepped up to the plate. My stepmother's mom decided to take me in. I moved to Tacoma to live with her, her husband, and her daughter. This turned out to be pure hell. The whole family was quite different, and impossible to get along with. I spent every day after school in my room or in the closet with an old computer in it. My school was seriously a ghetto school. The day before I began, some kid brought a gun to school for a drug deal. There were fights in the bathrooms everyday, and Cripts [sic] and Bloods roamed the school. *This was definitely not what I was used to. At Lakes High School, I learned that the only way I could survive was to be invisible. Each day was horrible, and I made only a few friends, who were mostly Cripts [sic]. I got tired of living in Tacoma, and after about two months, I finally stood up for myself. I left Tacoma, and since I had nowhere else to go, my mom had to take me back home, and for good this time.*

Part 6: The Beginning

I spent five years being unhappy. I have learned that happiness is a choice, and for the first time in as long as I can remember, I am finally a happy person. I am probably one of the few people you will meet that actually LIKES being at school. I wake up in the morning with a smile on my face, everyday, and every morning, I look forward to seeing the great friends I've finally made. I have learned to forgive both my parents in my heart, and for the first time in my life, things are working out. It was impossible to write about all the experiences I've had in all the places and schools I've been to, but just know that they are what have molded my life. I do not regret anything. All the people I've met, all the tears, laughter, joy, and yes, even sadness, are what have made me. And now it is time for my story to end, because we have finally reached the beginning.

Most of the content is familiar. Well-versed in the timeframe since my divorce, I've known my children's pain. It multiplies the depth of my guilt and regret. Maybe if I could have predicted the fallout, I would have waited until they left for college. I thought our lives would be better without the distress of an unhappy marriage. But Sarah's essay tells the story from her point of view—how she's lived through the turmoil of a divorce, moved to an unfamiliar place, and then, slowly adjusted to remarriages. Some of the content describes fond memories. Some describes painful, profound failures I would rather forget. Some is totally foreign. I can't deny the truth in her words.

"And now it is time for my story to end because we have finally reached the beginning," she writes. Now time has stopped for her. Time also stops for me. How little I really knew Sarah, and yet, how complete she feels her life had been. In many ways, this is the history of her life in her own words. I am so grateful to have it.

Curled on my daughter's rug, only the chirrups of frogs breaking through the silence, I imagine how it might be to face death. What happens? My mind pelts from question to question. If I let Sarah go, will she journey on toward the Light? Or has she already arrived where she is supposed to be? Where is she now? If I let go, will she somehow return to me in some way? I am not asking for life itself, but I am asking for something I can feel, some way that I can sense her, to know she hasn't left me forever.

tuesday, august 24

When the frogs quiet, time begins again for me. I haven't slept. But the shock of the previous twenty-four hours has been calmed by those seventeen words in the last sentence of Sarah's essay—*And now it is time for my story to end, because we have finally reached the beginning.*

Twenty-eight hours later, I write a short obituary. It isn't as straightforward as I expect. What a challenge. Who is Sarah? What is important to her? What photo suits her best? Where would she want donations to be sent? Should the obituary include extended family? How should I word a statement to indicate a private burial and a celebration of her life at the house, where everyone is welcome? I hammer out a rough draft.

> *Sarah Anne. Born February 5, 1988, in Seattle; died August 23, 2004, in a car accident on Bainbridge Island. Sarah was so full of love, life, and laughter and will be dearly missed by her family and many, many friends. Survived by her parents, Christopher J. and Caroline (and stepfather, Andy); twin sister, Caitlin; brother, Christopher; sisters, Mary and Anne; grandparents, Ed and Ginger, and Anita; great-grandparents, Duke and Orveline; uncles, Geordie and Jeff; aunt, Amie; and a large extended family and many friends. A celebration of Sarah's life*

will be held on Thursday, August 26, at 3 p.m. at her home.
Remembrances may be made to Bainbridge Education School
Trust or Children's Hospital & Medical Center, Seattle.

Whenever I pick up the morning paper, I read the obituaries, glancing at the photos, intrigued by the dates. When I see young people, I wonder how old they were. How did they die? Were they sick? Was there an accident? What were the details? And where did the donations go? Before today, when I read about a child or teenager or young soldier, I took a deep breath, thanked God that it wasn't my child, and offered up a prayer for the family who suffered. Now, as I read Sarah's obituary in Wednesday's paper, the prayer is for my family.

It is Tuesday, and I crave Christopher's presence. He is still in Montana with his father. I don't know why I haven't called him. I don't know what I can offer that will ease the hurt when I can't ease my own.

the last party

> *Somebody should tell us,*
> *right at the start of our lives, that we are dying.*
> *Then we might live life to the limit,*
> *every minute of every day.*
> *Do it! I say.*
> *Whatever you want to do, do it now!*
> *There are only so many tomorrows.*
>
> —Pope Paul VI

Sarah loved a good party, and this celebration is the last one she will ever have. It is her last hurrah, and I want it to be perfect. We gather in the kitchen with a few friends to plan. Father Quigg handles the formalities.

Andy heads up the work detail, designing a short leaflet outlining activities—readings, music, and poetry. He fusses over the yard and arranges for tents in case the weather changes, enough chairs for the older guests, a caterer and parking attendant, and housecleaners to do a quick shine. We prepare for a crowd of two hundred.

I want each guest to have a small, wallet-sized photo of Sarah, printed with the dates of her birth and death, along with her full name, Sarah Anne Gillette. Her name is important to me. I chose it. It is *Sarah* with an *h* and *Anne* with an *e*. *Ann* is my middle name, and I always wanted an *e* at the end. Now it is the first name of our youngest child.

In the midst of preparations, we create a new bedroom for Caiti down the hall from the other family bedrooms. She needs to be close to her surviving family, not isolated in the basement. And I want to be near her.

During the second afternoon, Caiti and Sarah's friends arrive. I encourage them to share in preparations for the party, recognizing, uncomfortable though it is, that they probably know her best.

One takes over the music, bringing his equipment, turning up the bass, softening the edge of the subwoofers, editing and testing the system, until he is sure the sound will vibrate through the forest. His ease with the shock soothes me.

A group of girls crafts poster boards, working with enthusiasm and care. I wonder how much thought they've given to the fragility of life—to thinking twice before taking chances, to understanding how their choices affect everyone around them. Right now, they obviously respect our grief.

For most of them, this is their first experience with death, and for many, the first time they have met Andy and me. My heart aches as I realize how hard it must have been for Caiti and Sarah when Andy wouldn't allow them to invite their friends over, even more because I didn't stand up for them. How will I greet her friends now, after missing the chance to know them while she lived?

As it happens, I am met with generosity and courage. Each friend, feeling this terrible loss, offers comfort. Some share words. Others share silence. Compassion flows from them. I gain more from their presence than from any medication a doctor could prescribe. I promise myself, then and there, that Christopher's friends will always be welcome in our home.

Leaving our house, some surely recognize they aren't invincible. I've overheard stories. Kids drinking until they throw up, then drinking more. Some using drugs. My kids are not immune. Boundaries sometimes fail. Substance abuse is a part of island culture—no different from any other community. Maybe this ugly accident will begin small changes, bring other parents to greater awareness, help shift things ... maybe.

Early Tuesday evening, arriving in a black suit draped over his lanky frame with a skinny black tie choking his long neck, a familiar face appears at the door to visit Caiti. I have never liked this boy. But here he is, eighteen years old, expressing his condolences. I wouldn't have thought he owned a suit. I have misjudged him.

By late Tuesday evening, I am inspired by teenagers and their friendship.

wednesday, august 25

Wednesday morning, Caiti and I wait for Christopher to get off the ferry. Spotting him in the crowd, I feel for the first time that something good might be possible, again.

Soon after we get home, the funeral director calls, asking if I'd like a few small containers of Sarah's ashes before the rest go into the urn. Hand-painted cloisonné boxes, an inch in diameter, are available in different colors. I order five; one for me; one for Caiti, one for Sarah's Nonny, one for her father in Montana, and one for her grandma in Manhattan.

On Bainbridge, gossip is flying. Eight teens involved in a midnight joyride in a small community. What were those kids thinking? Where were their parents? Why weren't they in their own beds? Who's at fault? Were drugs and alcohol involved? So many rumors, so few facts. Assumptions feed the editorials, gobbled up by readers of the local paper. Television crews from Seattle wait at the base of our driveway, pleading for interviews. Media reports are sensationalized. Heat flares among groups of kids, some sympathizing with the driver, some blaming her. Some whisper that the joy riders got what they deserved. Adult opinions also run the gamut. Only the seven survivors know the real story. And each tells it from a different, and personal, perspective. Sarah, sometimes joking, said she wanted to go out with a bang. She did just that.

The community is shaken. The island has been a cocoon of safety and security for decades. But, just two days earlier, another girl had died on the road, a nineteen-year-old whose better judgment wasn't with her that night. Then Sarah's accident, a vehicle filled with eight teenagers, also using very poor judgment. It pierces my heart that so many harsh judgments are passed by people who have certainly made their own mistakes.

A few nights later, a candlelight vigil is held at a local church, organized by a girl in Sarah's sophomore class. It is another warm August night. All ages attend—friends, parents, and kids. The crowd spills out the doorways. As they hold flickering candles, light spreads through the stained glass windows, casting radiance along the walkway and into the night. Andy and I sit in the parking lot, our grief too raw to share in public. The rest of our family stays home.

At our house, more flowers arrive, along with cards, calls, and emails. Sarah would have loved the attention. Staring at the front of our house, I realize the obituary should have read: "In lieu of flowers, please make a contribution to your local animal shelter." Sarah loves animals—dogs topping the list. But, as I said, there are no guidebooks to losing a child.

thursday, august 26

On the morning of Sarah's funeral, Mary and Annie stay home with a sitter while the rest of us catch an early ferry. The burial is set for 11:00 a.m., the celebration at 3 p.m. at our Bainbridge house. I ride in the passenger seat while Andy drives. In back, Caiti and Christopher sit in silence, staring out the windows. I envision Sarah sitting between them in the middle seat.

I wear a comfortable gray jersey skirt and matching top. Too afraid to look in the mirror, my face remains bare. I've dropped ten pounds in four days. I am forty years old.

The crossing to Seattle takes thirty-five minutes. This day, it feels like hours. On Monday, I mailed the check to the funeral home for their services. Today I pull out another blank check. The cemetery expects payment before the box containing Sarah's ashes can be deposited. I take a blue pen and slowly, in my best penmanship, fill in the blanks. I am paying for a plot of land where my dead child's remains will lie alongside the rest of her family.

I think about all the blessings I have taken for granted. I will never hold Caiti and Sarah together in my arms again, never feel our three hearts beating together. Sarah will never again burst through the front door. Children should not die before their parents and their grandparents and their great-grandparents. It is more painful than any parent should have to bear.

Arriving at the old cemetery, I walk into the business office to deliver the check. The manager introduces himself and hands me paperwork to sign. I note an additional amount already tallied into the total—$695.00, designated for lifetime care—such a small amount for a lifetime of tending. I would have been so grateful to spend the tens of thousands required to educate and care for her. I hand him the signed check. He says he'll mail copies for my files.

Calvary Cemetery

We park in the shade of the big Japanese maple and walk over to the green tent marking Sarah's gravesite, facing south, overlooking Lake Washington and Mount Rainer.

Nineteen years earlier, I'd stood in the rain watching as my Mimi's casket was slowly lowered into her grave. The rich, brown wood of that ornate box was so highly polished that the gray skies reflected off the curved lid. It was mid-November, my father's birthday. I rode from the cathedral to the cemetery in my uncle's Chevy Suburban, my oldest cousin following three black limousines and a motorcycle brigade. Willie Nelson played on the radio.

Eight years later, when the twins were four, we stood there again, as my Papa's ashes were placed next to his beloved wife. Papa was a loyal churchgoer in his own way. Every Sunday, without fail, while Mimi attended Mass, Papa parked his blue Chevy Celebrity station wagon in the loading zone and read the Sunday *Seattle Times* until she returned. He counted that as going to church.

For years, the twins and I visited the cemetery on holidays and birthdays to place flowers at the family plot. They never knew Mimi and barely knew Papa, but they had heard many family stories, told again and again. Now, I realize that Annie and Mary will know Sarah only through the stories we share of her.

> *Death is the opening of a more subtle life,*
> *In the flower, it sets free the perfume;*
> *in the chrysalis, the butterfly;*
> *In man, the soul.*
>
> —Juliette Adam

the funeral

Father Quigg greets us as we gather, smiling and wrapping his arms around me, taking Andy and Christopher into the group hug. Caiti walks in the opposite direction and sits down on the grass.

When Sarah's dad, Chris, and his family arrive, we are joined for a moment in unspeakable grief, exchanging hellos before forming a wide circle around the loamy mound. Mother and I flank Grandmom in her wheelchair. Christopher stands in front of me, Andy to my side. Caiti sits, Indian-style, picking blades of grass, eyes wide open, distracted. Chris's family stands across from us while friends fill in the empty spaces. The midday sun reflects off the plain, brown metal box containing Sarah's ashes—nine inches wide by nine inches deep by five inches high. I think, "This is all that's left of my child."

Grandmom sits with her back to the sun, her starched white hair cropped and styled. Even amidst great sadness, her beauty shines through. This death is not in the natural order of things—a child's lifetime cut short. She remembers a time in her own youth when her young, handsome fiancé had been killed in a similar accident. She grieves, not only for Sarah but also for those left behind to suffer the loss. Her pale blue eyes are blistered and reddened with tears. I wonder if she fears death.

Father Quigg's tears surprise me. He has performed so many funerals, with prayer and lighthearted humor to soften the grief, but Sarah's death in the bloom of her life is hard for him. And, they were friends.

Geordie reads the first prayer. Sometimes he drove Sarah to school, rap music booming through the speakers in his old van, windows rolled down, car thumping along, he and Sarah smiling and mouthing the words. My brother, Jeff, who survived shopping with Sarah for her freshman year prom dress, offers up the next reading. These uncles are Sarah's favorites.

Father Quigg reads the Gospel according to John, then continues into the homily, telling stories of Sarah that make everyone smile. Five months before, during a family wedding reception, as he sat, flanked on either side by the twins, Sarah leaned toward him with a big smile. "I have something to show you," she said, inching up her blouse to reveal the fighting Irishman. Laughter bellowed between the three of them, all ignoring my look of tight-lipped disapproval.

The story of that tattoo highlights the homily, twisted just a tad to make it more intriguing. Not only is Father Quigg a great storyteller; he also remembers the gift of life over the loss of death. His Irish brogue is a balm to my spirit.

Homily done, he lifts his right hand to bless the ashes, reciting, "In the name of the Father, the Son, and the Holy Spirit" while making the sign of the cross above the metal box as it is lowered into the open grave. The overall mood, lifted by the homily, turns somber.

Father Quigg invites us to place a memento in the open grave. My mother gently drops a photo of Caiti and Sarah as three year olds, wearing matching dresses of pink and white stripes, paired with navy blue sandals and lacy bobby socks, their mouths puckered as they stare into the camera.

Christopher bends low and drops in a bracelet Sarah had woven for him at summer camp. Fashioned of once-colorful cotton threads, it is tight for him now. He has worn it for four years.

My gift is a sterling silver bracelet, with SARAH engraved on the nameplate. Purchased as a Christmas present, it's been stashed in the back of my closet. I also drop a small photo of our family taken at a luau in Hawaii when I was eight months pregnant with Annie. I don't have a photo of all seven of us.

Caiti and Sarah, age 3

*Caiti, Andy holding Mary, Caroline, Sarah, Christopher,
November 2003*

Sarah's dad and others offer notes and photos and treasured items. A short metal shovel is passed around the circle to fill the grave.

Caiti sits very still, mounds of pulled grass flanking her knees. I kneel and take her in my arms, wiping her eyes, praying that time will heal her wounds.

As our family sings "Amazing Grace," the funeral director hands me a small sack containing the five boxes of Sarah's ashes, along with a sealed envelope containing two personal items removed from Sarah's body: a white metal nose ring and a belly ring with a clear stone.

After the service, dazed and dull, we walk to our cars and catch the ferry back to Bainbridge.

Sarah Anne Gillette   February 5, 1988 - August 23, 2004

celebrating sarah's life

Sarah's party begins. Everyone signs the guest book, taking Sarah's photo and a card memorializing her life. Some of the guests I know; most I don't. I wonder how many Sarah knows. The front lawn quickly fills to capacity, bulging out the sides of the oversized party tents, sprawling to the edge of the forest. I stand on the porch before the big door where just three days ago two strangers told us that Sarah would never come home.

While Caiti loses herself in the crowd, Christopher sits with his friends—ten- and eleven-year-old boys, dressed in polo shirts or button-down collars, wearing khakis or new jeans, and sneakers—huddling together on the porch steps, their soccer coaches framing the sides. Sarah's dad and his family find chairs.

Promptly at 3 p.m., the friend who'd organized the music steps up to the microphone and asks for silence. He hands me the microphone. Swallowing hard, I say, "Welcome. I'm Caroline, Sarah's mom. Thank you for coming to celebrate her life."

Father Quigg makes a few remarks. The music begins to play, starting with the "Hallelujah Song." I've requested a country song called, "When You Say Nothing at All." Sarah said she thought of me when it played on the radio. Most of the other music is rap or hip-hop, which I don't enjoy, but the kids do. Last up is Tupac's, "How Long Will They Mourn Me?"

The energy seems to rock the surrounding forest. People talk and laugh. Stories are told. A few friends ask if they can spend some time in Sarah's bedroom and understand when I politely refuse.

Midway through the party, three men walk across the lawn carrying musical instruments: one all in black, another wearing an old red T-shirt with a guitar on the front, a third man hanging behind and letting the other two talk. They are traveling from California to Canada and heard about Sarah on the ferry from Seattle. "Do you mind if we play some songs for Sarah?"

They play tunes from the eighties and nineties until the last stragglers leave. It is an unexpected tribute and one Sarah would have loved. I will always remember them.

Two hours after the party ends, a man walks through the open front door--a tall, well-dressed man in suit and dress shoes. "I'm sorry I missed Sarah's celebration. My daughter came. She was most touched. Thank you for sharing today with everyone." I've never seen that man again.

Another mother drops by: "Thank you for playing teenage music instead of music you would've preferred. You must be an amazing mother." She lives in town with her family. I've met her son a few times. Sarah's spent time in their basement, playing music too loud. I haven't forgotten her words.

Only three and a half days have passed since that terrible morning. It seems like years.

 *tolo road*

Oh, earth, you're too wonderful for anybody to realize you.
Do any human beings ever realize life while they live it—
every, every minute?

—Thornton Wilder
Our Town

Details of the accident on August 23, 2004, trickled in like drips from a broken faucet, a rumor here, a splash of truth there. In the days ahead, after seven teenagers were interviewed, the police investigation was completed and the police report sent to the prosecutor's office.

I have never read the paperwork and have asked few questions over the years. Too painful for me. In the days ahead, I gathered details of Sarah's final sixteen hours. This is how I imagine she would describe it.

Just an ordinary Sunday
August 22, 2004

Summer always ends too soon. Caiti and I were ready to enter junior year at the high school. We'd had a lot of chaos in the family when our parents divorced and both of them remarried. It was tough for all of us. My dad moved to Montana and my mom and stepdad, Andy, had two new babies. Caiti and I spent some time living with relatives and attending boarding schools for a couple of years till peace could be declared on the war front. But now, we were all back together—Mom and Andy, Caiti, Christopher, and me, and the babies. Christopher and Andy had been in Utah for a bicycle competition, and then

Christopher left for Montana to visit our dad for a week or so before school started.

That Sunday morning, we girls had the run of the house and spent it watching my favorite movie, Gone with the Wind, while the babies played around on the rug. Scarlett O'Hara was my kind of girl. When people in the family called me a fireball, I was being Scarlett. She said what she thought, lived without apology, and when something needed to get done, she did whatever it took. Scarlett was a survivor—just like me.

Caiti and I shared adjoining bedrooms in the daylight basement. We also had a big hanging-out room down there with sofas, the old console TV, and a Ping-Pong table. But, even though it was our designated space, Andy wouldn't let us have friends over without "giving advance notice," and even then, he usually said no. It was a sore point all around.

But, that day, we huddled happily on the sofa under an old blue blanket, rocking the little ones in our laps when they got tired and passing bowls of popcorn loaded with melted butter and salt. I had a warm, weird feeling that afternoon, but I wasn't sick, so I let it go.

When the movie was over, Caiti and I cranked up the volume on a favorite song by The Cure, "Just like Heaven," singing the lyrics as loud as we could and dancing.

When the party broke up, I started a campaign to spend the night at a friend's house. Mom wasn't for it, but I argued her down until she caved and let me go.

Late that afternoon, Caiti and I jumped into the old Jeep Wrangler that Mom gave us after Caiti got her license. (I hadn't bothered to get my license yet, but I figured there was plenty of time.) Caiti and I took off the doors and the canvas top, so even though it sputtered and stalled on cold mornings, our old Jeep could cruise.

Before we left the house, I grabbed a box of Stouffer's Macaroni & Cheese from the freezer, grabbed the DVD of Gone with the Wind, and jammed the cell phone into my back pocket. I thought about going back for my wallet, but I didn't need it. I'd be home the next morning.

"I love you, Mama," I said, waving goodbye. She stood at one end of the kitchen, feeding rice cereal to my littlest sister in her bouncy chair. (I'd always wanted to dance across that concrete slab topping the large island in the center of our kitchen, like in the movies.) Annie flailed her arms, and the chair bounced; my other little sister, Mary, stood in her walker while Mom loaded Cheerios in her tray. I breezed out of there, blowing Mom a kiss, and wiggling my fingers at the babies. Caiti dropped me off at Connor's and went back home to help with dinner.

Connor was a good friend—not a boyfriend. Since sixth grade, when I was the new girl in school, he had included me in his crowd. He was easy with himself, and I liked the smell of his hair—Herbal Essence Shampoo. For the past two years, I'd dyed my dirty blond strands the same dark brown as his. At school, I'd watch him sail across the soccer field, making my skills look pitiful. Most of the time, I felt more welcomed at his house than my own.

I popped the Macaroni & Cheese into the microwave. Later, we—Connor, his mother, his sister, and I—planted ourselves in front of the wide-screen TV to watch Gone with the Wind. (Perfect! Twice in one day!) Even with everything cozy and safe, that strange warm feeling came over me again.

Our houses were separated by less than three miles. Only one stop sign. No traffic lights. My house on the south end of Bainbridge Island, Connor's in the middle. It was the last night of my life—August 22, 2004. Before daybreak, I would die.

For sure, I didn't see the end coming.

About 11:30 that night, I was dozing on the sofa when my cell phone rang. The ring tone was Billy Joel's "Only the Good Die Young"—the one I'd assigned to my sister.

"Whad up?" I said.

"Just lyin' in bed, listening to my iPod. You okay?" She listened to the same ten songs, over and over. I knew her playlist.

"Yeah, I was almost asleep. Tired."

"You sure? I can come get you. I'm just lying here doing nothing."

I could hear her throat twitching, almost feel her palms sweat and her eyelids flutter, her lips tense, like before an exam at school. When anxiety set in, the weird quirks started. And since our parents' divorce and all the trouble that came after it, she could get really anxious. But I knew she'd get over it. In fact, I loved that about her, just as I loved the high heels she wore to school and the miniskirts she bought at Forever 21 and her passion for all things pink.

That wasn't for me, though. I wore jeans and tennis shoes and T-shirts.

"I'm gonna jump in the extra bed here," I said. "Come get me in the morning. Sleep tight."

"I love you," we said at the same moment and giggled.

Caiti and I were best friends one minute and fought like mean girls the next. But that didn't matter 'cause our last goodnights were always to each other. We were twins—two sides of the same coin.

Monday
August 23, 2004

It was an hour or so after midnight when Connor woke me up, definitely past my curfew of 11:30. Another boy had stopped by after I went to sleep, and they stayed up surfing the Web and instant messaging.

"Ya wanna go to Safeway for some snacks?" I was always up for food and a good time. I borrowed five bucks and went out to the Ford Explorer waiting in the driveway.

I knew the girl driving the car, but I didn't know the girl in the passenger seat. As it turned out, they were only fourteen. They sort of looked alike, with long brown hair and lots of makeup and mascara. They definitely knew how to work the junior boys already in the middle seats.

Connor opened the rear hatch and climbed into one of the jumper seats. Another boy followed, and then I crawled in. Since I was the last one, I sat down on Connor's lap, and we pulled the hatch closed. The car was a mess inside, littered with McDonald's bags and empty soda cans and torn candy wrappers.

At the store, we stocked up on chips, sodas, candy, chocolate milk, a turkey sandwich, and a pint of chocolate ice cream. Loaded down with our junk food, we hopped into the SUV and took off.

Who was in the car? Two fourteen-year-old girls driving without driver's licenses, five boys over sixteen with driver's licenses, and I, just sixteen, with a driver's permit. Makes you wonder, doesn't it?

One of the younger girls said she had to return a pair of borrowed gym shorts somewhere on the west side of the island, so we headed in that direction. We crossed High School Road, turned right on Miller, and stopped at the intersection of Tolo Road. Tolo was narrow and hilly, like a roller coaster. It had a reputation, called "doing the Tolo." Picking up speed, the car would catch air at the top of the hill. When all four wheels left the road, your body sprang up, and your head grazed the roof. When the wheels slammed back down on the road, you were slammed back into your seat. It was my first time.

Hailey, the girl who'd taken her parents' car, was the driver. She stopped in the middle of the road, flipped off the headlights, and killed the engine. Everything went black.

"Anybody want out?" she asked. "Now's your chance."

We could've gotten out then—should have, would have— but we didn't.

With the car lights off, it was really dark. Big trees and long ditches lined both sides of the road.

Silence. Everybody scared but excited. When Hailey stomped the accelerator, Connor cinched his arms tight around my waist, so tight I could hardly breathe. I gripped the edge of the seat with clammy palms. Tolo Road was less than a mile long, less than two miles from Connor's house, less than four miles from my house, less than five minutes from being safe.

After the first run, Hailey stopped the car for a minute, looked back at us passengers, put her right foot back on the gas pedal, and took a sharp right turn onto Battle Point Drive. A few grumbled curses broke the silence. I took a deep breath. The borrowed gym shorts were flung over a mailbox.

Then, she headed back to Tolo Road and cut the engine. The unspoken challenge hung heavy in the air. The girls swapped seats.

Most of us in the rear thought one time of "doing the Tolo" was enough for one night. The language got ugly. Some of the kids wanted out. I didn't turn to look at Connor. My eyes stayed on the girls changing seats.

It was so dark, you could hardly see your hands in front of your face, and we hadn't passed another car since leaving Safeway. It was 1:35 in the morning. No cell phone service. Trees blocked the coverage. If we got out of the car, we'd have at least a two-mile walk to get home. Worst of all, we'd never live it down.

The second girl, Hannah, took the wheel in both hands and stomped down hard on the gas. The car shot off, rough and unsteady. At eighty-five miles an hour, in the last quarter mile stretch, the front tire clipped the edge of the road, and the car went out of control, flipping over, righting itself, and finally, smashing into a huge tree. Rubber and metal screeched on the oily pavement, making a sickening sound. Echoes. Burning rubber. Nausea. Neck snapping. The back of my head was crushed against the car frame. I smelled oil dripping on the ferns. Heat from the underside warmed my back. A sharp light radiated through the smoke rising from the car. I felt nothing. Numb.

A boy in one of the middle seats freed himself and stumbled off to find help. Neighbors came running down their driveways with flashlights. They were used to the hollow screeches and the smell of burning rubber, but not this. Never this.

Unless you stood in front of the mangled car, you couldn't see anything. All you could do was follow the screams.

It was like a movie set, like something awful being filmed. EMTs and firefighters showed up, sirens blaring, lights flashing. Neighbors did whatever they could, bringing battery-powered spotlights, blankets and towels, chainsaws, comforting words. Ambulances roared up. People were shouting orders. A flight-for-life helicopter landed at the fire station helipad. Somebody called the coroner.

Parents of the seven survivors were called right away. But my family slept on.

The two drivers—Hailey and Hannah—walked away with a few bruises, one with a broken arm. Their parents drove them to the local clinic. A few hours later, they went home.

The three boys in the middle seat had mild head injuries, one broken leg, and some cuts and bruises. Their parents followed the ambulances as they were rushed to the nearest hospital, a good forty-minute drive without traffic. About six hours later, they were all asleep in their beds.

The boy in the right jumper seat was badly hurt. Several organs were punctured and both legs injured. He was airlifted *to Harborview Medical Center in Seattle and hooked up to a ventilator.*

After the accident, Connor's arms still cinched my waist. A firefighter pulled them away and removed him from the wreckage. The femur in his left leg was shattered in several places. He had head injuries and bad cuts across his face and neck. An ambulance rushed him to the second helicopter. After four days in intensive care and several surgeries, he was released. Twice a week for the next year, he had physical therapy to regain full motion of his leg. Several plastic surgeries repaired some of the scarring on his face and neck.

Connor would spend over two years in therapy to help him come to terms with what happened. No way could he have known that every day of his life when he looked in the mirror, the deep scars on his neck and left side of his face would remind him of Tolo Road. Physically, he got better. He lived. Getting over it … I don't know.

As for me, my skull was shattered, crushed from behind. My face wasn't injured. I wasn't mangled. There wasn't much blood. One of the emergency workers, a stepfather of a girlfriend, recognized me and gently removed my body from the wreckage, attending to my needs. Even in death, we need to be cared for.

My cell phone was still in my back pocket. If I'd had my wallet, they'd have seen that I was an organ donor. Maybe something of mine—a kidney, my heart, maybe my blue eyes—could have made a difference in some other teenager's life.

The accident happened at 1:42 a.m., Monday, August 23, 2004.

Death doesn't happen instantly. For a little while, you hover around your body, confused. What you want more than anything is to go home, to be safe, to know you're okay. But my life was over.

the days

The days come and go, but they say nothing,
and if we do not use the gifts they bring,
they carry them as silently away.

—Ralph Waldo Emerson

*I*crawled into bed that Thursday, August 26, just before midnight, taking note of my physical changes. My head felt crushed in a vise, turning slowly, a quarter turn every half-hour. The elastic band on my pajama bottoms fell below my waist, cuffs dragging on the floor. The babies seemed heavier, my son's head more weighted against my chest, body frozen as if sheathed in a straightjacket. It hurt to move.

Mary and Annie tucked in their cribs, Christopher and I recited his nightly prayers and said goodnight. Walking the ten steps to Caiti's room, I knocked and let myself in. We listened to the same song six times before saying goodnight. I'd never heard it before.

Today, when I turn on the radio and hear Jimmy Eat World's "Hear You Me," I return to that night, and the many nights when that song was played again and again, Caiti barely holding on, and remembering how grateful I was to find her alive the next morning. These are memories I wish I could forget.

In our bedroom, Andy snored lightly. The songs of toads and spring peepers wafted through the open windows. Some nights, the frog sounds and foghorns melded together like calls from ships lost at sea. Some nights, I didn't notice them. Some nights, they stole my sleep. Flickering lights from passing ferries sparkled through the evergreens between our house and Rich Passage below. Tonight, as I stared into the dark woods, the shadows of tall western red cedars reached for the moon.

Four days. The death. The burial. And now, a new chapter in life, one I never wanted or expected, one I couldn't yet imagine. My heart ached. Sarah's heart still beat within me.

Unable to sleep, or even rest, the longer I lay still, the more my muscles hardened. Pain shot through my limbs like lightning bolts. Electric shocks stung my scalp. My mind raced, questioned, and twisted like a knotted braid, as I tried to make sense of it all. But nothing made sense.

friday, august 27

Friday morning, I opened the door to Sarah's room and breathed it in. Emmett's hind leg rested on her favorite T-shirt—black with short sleeves and large white letters across the front—CBGB—tossed on the floor, waiting to be washed. I didn't remember buying it for her. Lifting it to my damp cheek, I smelled my daughter, so regretting the anger and nagging that had stolen so much of our precious time together.

Would Caiti die of a broken heart? Would stress destroy us? I couldn't let my own despair submit to sickness. The compassion in Emmett's eyes seemed to understand my concerns.

Picking up a perfectly round, etched bottle of Chanel Chance, I sprayed a light stream across my left wrist, and closed my eyes to inhale the misty particles of jasmine and citrus. I hadn't bought this for Sarah. Another heart-shaped bottle from the Escada Collection went on my right wrist. I wondered if the perfumes were fakes or gifts or prizes from some friend's shoplifting habit. Sarah had sworn to me she'd never shoplifted. I believed her.

My sense of smell unlocks memories I would otherwise never recall, even those I would rather forget.

Sarah's round, wooden hairbrush captured strands of hair in the nylon bristles. With both hands, I clutched her baby blanket, now just a yellow cotton remnant, frayed at the edges, spotted with black mascara and eyeliner, unwashed for several years. Sixteen years ago, it was beautiful—hand-quilted, with peach accents and white piping, embroidered with her initials, S A G, in the bottom left corner. Using Grandmom's old Singer and her wooden embroidery frames, I had fashioned the quilt on a lopsided cardboard table in our small apartment below the Pike Place Market. It had worn well.

With Emmett beside me, I eased down onto Sarah's lambskin rug, siting Indian-style. She had asked for the rug to be her main Christmas gift when she was eleven. It was nothing special, just another bulk-warehouse item that anyone could buy. It lay on the left side of her bed closest to the row of windows overlooking my prized perennials. I remembered now that during the four weeks before the accident, even though his hip dysphasia made it tricky to use those steep basement stairs, I'd often found Emmett strewn across the cushy lambskin. Now, I wondered if he had a sense of what was coming. Who knows?

Emmett nuzzled his heavy square head into my lap. This big, old lab weighed in at over 115 pounds, more than me. He came to us as a puppy when the twins were five and Christopher was a baby. Always at my heels, always my companion, we took long walks on the nearby trails at Fort Ward State Park and drove the island roads together. Every night, I removed his faded blue nylon collar as if preparing a child for bed and, every morning, put it back around his thick neck. I considered him a best friend.

Leaving Sarah's bedroom, I closed the door, off-bounds now to everyone, except Caiti and Christopher. Except for once in October, it would be more than ten months before I felt emotionally strong enough to open this door again.

saturday, august 28

By Saturday afternoon, after all the intensity and hard work, the house fell silent, as though life had come to a complete halt. And it had. No urgent tasks, no deadlines, no sense of purpose. We were stuck in a thick, dense fog, moving in slow motion, or not at all.

The father of the teenage driver, Hannah, called to say that his daughter wanted to apologize and asked if they could visit. They had not attended our celebration for Sarah. I invited them to come Saturday night at eight o'clock.

The babies were put to bed early. Christopher went upstairs to play computer games. Caiti was out with friends. She didn't need to know that the girl who'd killed her twin sister was in our home. I didn't tell her. Watching as Hannah's father parked his shiny Lexus SUV, I placed him in his upper fifties, tall and thin, with glasses and a receding hairline of gray-blond hair. He introduced the family at the door, and Andy and I did our best to put them at ease. Before this night, we'd never seen them.

Hannah wore a dark skirt and white blouse, her long brown hair pulled back. Her face was healthy and free of makeup. She looked to her father for reassurance. I wasn't sure how I imagined she would look, but she looked fourteen.

Hannah's mother, several years younger than her husband, dressed simply, her face drawn tight. She shuffled in, shoulders bent, her head down. For a moment, we stood quiet and awkward. "I'm so sorry," she said.

As we took our seats, Hannah pulled a frayed, folded sheet of notebook paper from her pouch and, looking down, began to read her letter of apology—a practiced speech, obviously sincere. Reflecting later, I couldn't remember anything about it.

Hannah would be a freshman at Bainbridge High School, where Sarah would have been a junior. She couldn't possibly grasp the grief that engulfed my family, the agony of Caiti's broken heart, the loss suffered by a ten-year-old brother. Hannah didn't get behind the wheel with the intention of killing someone. Perhaps, someday, she would understand the enormity of what had happened, but today, she was only fourteen.

I couldn't imagine that Sarah would have wanted this girl to bleed with guilt. I doubted Caiti would agree. But that Saturday night, I thanked God Sarah was not this girl. And I thanked God I was not that mother.

I thought I would never forget that family sitting across from us in our living room, their daughter reading her well-practiced apology. Today, even though I think of them often, I wouldn't be able to pick them out in a crowded room.

The next day, Sunday afternoon, a woman parked her car at the base of our cul-de-sac, and walked the gravel driveway along our split rail fencing to our front yard. She hadn't seen me watching from Mary's bedroom window. Wanting to keep the house quiet, I met the woman below the front steps. She introduced herself as the attorney for the girl who'd killed Sarah. Her introduction caught me off-guard. I was certain she'd spent the day with her client. Now here she was at the victim's home, trying to read my family.

"I wanted to come and apologize. I am so sorry. How are you doing? Is there anything I can do to help?" She spoke slowly, her hands clasped together--almost as in prayer. She looked into my eyes as if she felt my pain, the tone in her voice soft and solicitous. She was pleasant, in her mid-thirties. I wondered if she was a mother. If so, her child couldn't be that old.

The Kitsap County prosecutor later told us she was from a well-known firm in Seattle that represented persons convicted of white-collar crimes. I've never forgotten the look on her face as she asked how she could help my family. I have always appreciated her concern.

The last days of summer before school started, Caiti and her friends went to the crash site daily and found gifts and mementos. A notebook was left for visitors to leave thoughts and condolences. "Learn 2 Live,

Live 2 Love," boldly written with a black Sharpie across the front page. Caiti brought it home to share with me. I have it, still.

The crash site on Tolo Road

the weeks

*Faith is taking the first step even when you don't see
the whole staircase.*

—Martin Luther King Jr.

early september, year one

I called Verizon and canceled Sarah's cell phone.

Condolence gifts continued to arrive well into the second week: flowers and phone messages, casseroles, soups and stews, homemade desserts. We were overwhelmed with gratitude.

A handwritten note, sent from a sharp, kind, and inquisitive girl who befriended Sarah when we first moved to Bainbridge was tucked into an ivory card graced with a watercolor of a bare branch and several pink blossoms. She wrote fondly of a project she and Sarah had worked on together and ended the note by saying she'd miss Sarah in her classes. The letter cradled a memory.

I took a deep breath as I read. The memory shared was something I knew nothing about. I realized two things: once again, how much I didn't know about my daughter and how much I cherished in memories of her.

A week later, a small white votive was delivered. The card read, "Place this candle in your kitchen and light it each night. The candlelight is symbolic of your child's presence at the dinner table with your family." A beautiful thought.

I bought a frame made of white abalone shells, inserted my favorite photo of Caiti and Sarah, and placed it in the kitchen window with the candle. The photo was from our trip to Hawaii the previous fall. Purple and white leis drape the girls' necks, Sarah's head tilting forward, a goofy smirk on her face. Both girls stare into the lens of my camera. Mary was a baby then, and I was pregnant with Annie. Sarah would die in less than a year.

Caiti and Sarah, Hawaii, November 2003

School started two weeks after the accident. The tension on campus was thick, the hallways soaked in retaliation. Groups of high schoolers had clearly taken sides, some raging against the drivers, some sympathizing with them. Vicious voicemails littered cell phones. Houses were egged. One day, photos of the drivers, scantily clad and horsing around—which they had posted on their MySpace pages—blanketed the windshields in the high school parking lot. Within a month, both girls transferred to other schools.

During the weeks ahead, we gradually returned to our routines. I didn't want our home to become a shrine to the dead, but a place for the living to thrive. The shining candle in the kitchen was our altar. That was enough.

I taped Sarah's photo in the corner of my car's windshield so I could see her smiling down at us. I hoped her smile would remind the driver to be cautious and alert.

A few favorite photos were taped to a shelf in my bedroom closet, one of Sarah lying on a log at the beach when she was fourteen. She looked like a model in a teenage magazine, hair flung to one side as if she'd just awakened for the day and her familiar "see if I care" smirk. Another showed the twins on a beach in California, Sarah wearing her favorite black tee with CBGB across the front. Sarah would be the first child I said hello to each morning and the last goodnight.

Sarah in her CBGB shirt

Two families involved in the accident reached out to us. Five of the families made no contact. Some people approached us, not knowing what to say but there to help. Some offered advice. Some sent stories of the fourteen-year-olds tootling around the island in the family car, some indicating that they may have been given parental permission. Naturally, some in the community labeled me a bad mother and turned their backs. A few friendships dissolved. "Don't take it personally" became my motto—not that it made me feel any better.

Everyone was in crisis. Caiti questioned not how she would live but whether she wanted to live at all. For Christopher, the challenge was processing such a huge loss at such a young age. For Andy, the task was avoiding conflict and confusion, smothering the negativity. Sarah's grandmother, Nonny, sought accountability. I worried that Caiti might die of a broken heart and that our family would fall apart under the weight of this tragedy. I focused on how we would survive intact, as a family.

In the weeks ahead, I was especially concerned for Connor and his family. As I watched Caiti slipping further away, I knew he had to be facing his own demons. I tried to imagine living with memories of that night—memories of a friend sitting in your lap, held tightly against your chest, then suddenly gone forever. Blame couldn't be placed, nor judgments passed, between our family and his. It could easily have been our house from which Sarah and Connor left late that night, unknown to us.

Connor was still in intensive care when we celebrated Sarah's life. I knew he would have appreciated the outpouring of compassion that filled the forest that afternoon. I hoped that when sadness came to him—expectedly or unexpectedly or in great waves—Sarah would brush her fingertips over his scars like the fluttering of butterfly wings. I wanted to imagine he'd smile as the tension lifted from his broken body.

Ten days after Sarah was buried, I stood at Connor's family's front door with a bouquet of white roses. An older man answered my knock, probably the grandfather. I didn't introduce myself, and he didn't ask.

After exchanging a few words, I handed him the roses and drove home. Over the weeks ahead, Connor's mother and I became friends. She continues to honor Sarah's life—birthday cards in February, cards of remembrance every August, fresh flowers at the cemetery, a smile and "How are you?" when we meet in town.

Our home became my retreat. There was plenty to do. Each of my children had different needs. And I felt Sarah still had needs. Responsibility for her life hadn't ended just because she was dead. Her life's details needed tending. Her memory needed nurturing.

Avoiding reminders of Sarah was terribly hard. Everywhere I went, memories were waiting. Of course, I avoided the obvious. I didn't drive Tolo Road and detoured around the high school. Watching teenagers cross campus, get lunch at Safeway, or drive out of the parking lot was much too painful. Neither of my teenagers was in class. One was dead, the other unable to get out of bed. Suddenly, twins seemed to be everywhere. I avoided running into people by running errands at odd hours.

Andy took the ferry each morning for his consulting job in Seattle. As part of a team that organized think tanks for large companies, his life was very different from mine, and he was spending less and less time at home. He kept his emotions safe inside and wanted me to do the same. We never discussed Sarah's death. Never.

Andy's mother was forty-six when he was born; his father, fifty, already retired and ready to begin the second half of his life. With six siblings no longer living at home, he was raised as an only child in a quiet routine. He was close to his parents, sharing dinner with them three times every week, even after he reached adulthood. His dad died when Andy was twenty-eight, his mother, when he was thirty-four. A few of his friends had also died young. He shielded himself from these early losses by remaining slightly detached—caring, but not intimate. Andy had learned to avoid turmoil and confrontation, and

I was certainly in turmoil and grief, so instead of pulling together, we struggled separately to stay afloat.

In mid-September, the death certificate arrived.

> *Date of death: August 23.*
> *Hour of Injury: 0140+/-*
> *Immediate Cause: Multiple Blunt Force Injuries to the*
> *Head, Neck, and Chest*
> *Interval between Onset & Death: Brief*

I held it in my hands, reading and rereading, until I had memorized every word and punctuation mark. I continued to wait for the toxicology report.

fall, year one

> *Adopt the pace of nature; her secret is patience.*
> —Ralph Waldo Emerson

My mother was a pillar of strength during those lonely weeks and months, always available to talk and to help with the kids. She worried about my health.

I had not regained the ten pounds lost before the funeral, and arthritis ate at my joints. If I stopped moving, my muscles stiffened into solid bars. Pain consumed my body, radiating down one leg and up the other, from one hand across my shoulders and down the other arm, up my right side, back down my left side. I slept very little, less than three hours at a time, even with medication. My cropped hair sprouted gray and littered the tub when I shampooed. I hardly recognized the woman staring back at me in the mirror, as wrinkles scattered outward from the corners of my mouth, crackled along my upper lip, and spread over my forehead like shattered ice. It would be four years before I could read a book, focus, and recall the chapter just read.

Of course, well-meaning friends and family suggested therapy, but I had always been hesitant and uncertain about it. Caiti was unwilling to go, and the rest of the family, reluctant. We made a halfhearted attempt. After three sessions, I realized that we were not ready to add an unfamiliar process into our lives while we were scrambling with so many changes.

Somehow, we forged ahead.

Almost a month after Sarah died, the toxicology report arrived. The rumors were wrong. Sarah was tested for alcohol, opiates, cocaine, amphetamines, PCP, marijuana, methadone, propoxyphene, benzodiazepines, barbiturates, and tricyclic antidepressants. The report concluded: "You will find that the tests done have proved negative."

It didn't mean that Sarah would come home again or watch her favorite movies or plan for college. But it put to rest the illusion that many parents hide behind, that this incident and others like it were the result of "crazy teenagers making decisions that could never touch us." Instead, it was a momentary, late-night impulse that any teenager could make ... anywhere and at any time. Nonetheless, the debate continued in the local paper. Where were all those parents that night? Probably in bed sleeping, just like me. I canceled our weekly subscription.

There were parents who came forward to offer support. Those who had also lost children assured me that there was no right way or wrong way or timeline for grieving. They knew, as I would learn, that loss is very personal, that we each have to make it through in our own way and in our own time. Grief has no easy definition. Had I lost my child? I wasn't sure *lost* was the right verb.

Caiti and Sarah bathing Emmett, Summer 2002

Six weeks after Sarah's accident, Emmett died. Emmett had been a member of the family since Caiti and Sarah were five. He was eleven years old now. That wonderful sense of play now ceased, it seemed as if his big shoulders and splayed hips had absorbed the heaviness of Sarah's death. A cancer, probably growing awhile, had enveloped his body like a rain cloud. On good days, I wanted to believe his condition would improve. But I knew he suffered patiently, giving us time to say goodbye. Every morning, I walked him to the edge of the lawn and waited while he searched for a spot to relieve himself, then guided him back to his foam pad under the shade of the eaves. Every day, I sat on the green sofa, watching him, his eyes drinking in my eyes, his big head nudging mine as if he wanted me to stay alert, stay awake.

The day came too soon. "Nothing can be done," the vet said, staring at his black leather walking shoes. "What would you like to do?"

I wrapped my arms around his thick neck and unclasped his blue collar. I wondered if Sarah missed her dog. I prayed for Emmett to find her. Again, a devastating loss overwhelmed our house.

Miracles do not, in fact, break the laws of nature.

—C. S. Lewis

That night I lay awake, gazing at the forest outside. I felt a warmth surge through my toes, foot muscles massaged. I swore Sarah's hands held my cracked and weary feet. I felt the sweep of her hair brush my calves, a tickle on an insole. The light of the bedside clock reflected in the mirror beyond. I imagined her standing there in the white oversized T-shirt she'd worn to bed, eyes connecting with mine, smiling. Her presence didn't startle me. I expected her. The warmth was familiar, like the warmth I'd felt that Sunday morning when we watched *Gone with the Wind*. It passed over my face as though she were leaving a kiss on my cheek, trailing toward the moonlight, streaming across the bedroom carpet. The small round cloisonné container holding her ashes sat on the dresser near the foot of my bed. Somehow my daughter lived within me.

A week after Emmett's death, I announced to Andy, "Either we get a new dog, or we get a divorce." Though he was sure I'd gone mad, he agreed and drove Caiti and Christopher to see a litter of yellow labs. It was the first time the three had been alone together since that long drive to the cemetery. They brought home a small yellow female that immediately brought giggles and smiles into our house. She wrestled with Christopher on the lawn and snuggled with Caiti while she slept. The heavy air began to lift, just a little. Seven weeks had passed.

"Lady" was a diversion for me. She took snacks from my hand, slowly and appreciatively. Her graceful movements reminded me of the cocker spaniel in the Disney film, *Lady and the Tramp*. Andy and the kids didn't like the name "Lady." So, they called her "Brooke." I still call her "Lady." They still call her "Brooke." The dog deals with it.

The puppy paused my days as I noted the small things that mattered. Maybe tomorrow wouldn't come. I knew truth in that, and recognized the present, as a *present*. Weeks ticked past as if from an old clock requiring daily winding, the key hidden in some remote rear pocket. I had to search to find it.

Lady Brooke

When I was a child, our family had a black toy poodle named Pepe and two English springer spaniels. My children had Labradors, chocolate and black, sometimes one, sometimes two. From the animals, the kids learned trust, patience, and friendship. They learned about fair play. Humans have much to learn from dogs.

how can you tell them apart?

People often asked this about the twins. When they were babies, wet in the tub, I'd search for the small triangular birthmark on the back of Sarah's left leg. When they were preteens, straight from bed or wet from the shower, I'd do a double take. When they were teenagers, I listened to the words as they danced off Caiti's tongue or curled off Sarah's lips. I knew who was who.

But to separate feelings for a child who was dead from a twin who barely seemed alive—that was an endless obstacle course. Death was raw and life was confusing. I struggled with both.

Sometimes, I felt Sarah wanted Caiti to herself—as if Sarah wasn't ready to be alone either. Certainly, Caiti wasn't ready to leave Sarah. It was in her sleep, in her dreams, that life for Caiti felt normal, whatever that meant.

Watching Caiti move and talk kept Sarah nearer. I found comfort in the blue of Caiti's eyes, sometimes carrying me to another place.

Sometimes the similarities overwhelmed—almost as overwhelming as the pandemonium in our house. I missed Sarah so much. She was my child, and here was another child, Caiti—so similar to her, alive and in front of me. Again, I forlornly retreated to gratitude that I hadn't lost two children in one night.

In late October 2004, the prosecution charged the teenage driver who had caused the accident. Having sped down Tolo Road, exceeding the speed limit by more than fifty miles per hour, she pled guilty to two counts: driving without a license and vehicular homicide. Before a packed courtroom, she said, "On August 23, 2004, I drove a car without thinking about the safety of others." Sentencing was set for December 7.

Christopher celebrated his eleventh birthday four weeks after the accident. He resembled Sarah in many ways: smart and streetwise with a comfortable sense about himself and the same streak of humor.

Each morning, I drove Christopher to school and watched him move easily into his crowd, a collection of young boys. They seemed immune to the rumors and judgments blowing through our community, keeping busy with school and extracurricular activities, avoiding the drama. Christopher didn't bother with the "whys" or "what if's." He didn't need to blame someone for his sister's death.

At that time, I believed these boys would still be Christopher's good friends when he was sixteen, a junior in high school. Today, I know that as true. Growing up on Bainbridge Island—a contained community—does have many advantages.

We arrived at school each morning about twenty-minutes early so I wouldn't need to wave and smile, watching all the parents dropping their kids off, the ones who would come back home safe and sound that afternoon. Sometimes, I unfolded my plaid blanket at the end of the soccer field to watch Christopher's games, keeping my distance from the other moms and dads, who predictably respected my distance. It seemed some were afraid, as though death might be contagious.

Each night, Christopher and I prayed for Sarah, for kindness among all children, and thanked God for our blessings. I'd brush his blond curls to the right, plant a kiss, and quietly shut his bedroom door behind me, just as I'd done since he was a baby. Then, I'd go to Caiti's room.

One night, about three months after the accident, I heard faint sniffles and saw a dim light beneath Christopher's door. Quietly, I let myself in and sat on the side of his bed. His room felt warm, not like the stuffiness of a baby's room, but like a warm, still day at the beach. Clenching his baby blanket in both arms, my son cried.

Haltingly, he began, "Mom, I don't remember the last time I saw Sarah. Where were we? What did we do?" Since he was in Montana when she died, we had to think back to a family dinner before Christopher and Andy left for the bike trip to Utah. I had served pasta with pesto sauce.

He continued, "Mom, nobody asks me how I'm doing."

That was true. Everyone was deeply concerned about Caiti but Christopher seemed unscathed by it all, so we assumed that he was. And I had never asked. "I don't remember Sarah's laugh." He looked at me, wanting answers. Sarah had always called him, "My little man." But he didn't remember that or anything else about her, so different from Caiti, living only in her memories.

Here I was again, not knowing what to say or do. Certainly, I couldn't change, or even explain, what had happened. But there was something I could do. I could start talking, push back the hidden recesses that kept me pretending to all who asked, "Oh, I'm fine, I'm okay," while I was dying inside. A torrent of rain beat against the bedroom window.

I took Christopher in my arms, embracing my son's pain, his search to know his sister, his need to fill in the blanks that should have been filled with memories. I'd never realized how important she was to him.

Suddenly, I was furious with Sarah. She had put all of us in this terrible position. Why didn't she consider her family before getting into that car?

Christopher stayed home from school the next day, his first absence since starting kindergarten. Together we went downstairs to Sarah's room. Lady forged through and flopped down on the lambskin rug. I waited at the door while Christopher went inside. Till that moment, I had lacked the strength to open that door. But now, I had a reason: to help my son deal with his grief.

On that rainy, cold day, not one ray of light fell across Sarah's desk. The garden had died. Christopher sat at his sister's desk, where she did homework each night. I stroked the puppy's round belly.

The desktop was dusty. Magazines littered the surface. A pile of favorite books sat next to the windowsill—*The Chosen, The Great Gatsby, The BFG, Lilly's Purple Plastic Purse.* Sarah's perfume and hairbrush lay in the brown wicker tray. Several photos sat on the windowsill. One showed all three kids on an airboat during a family trip to the Florida Keys when Christopher was just four years old, all three sunburned and smiling. Another photo taken on a recent trip to Canada. Another of our annual Easter egg hunts, scrambling for the golden egg. Tears welted the skin of his checks like the rain dripping from the gutters, his blue eyes threaded by red vessels.

Florida Keys, May 1997

Opening the desk drawers, he discovered the letters he'd written to Sarah at summer camp when he was five. His printing was a little hard to read, but the letters had made it to the camp's mailbox. Each letter had been opened, returned to its envelope, and saved. Pink rubber bands grouped the letters in piles, one stack from each summer. Sarah had saved every letter.

Visiting Sarah at Four Winds Camp, July 1999

He stood up and walked the few steps to study the tousled white cotton sheets of her bed and lay his head on her pillow, his chest rising and falling, his eyes closing for a few minutes, breathing in Sarah's scent.

Afterward, he selected a few mementos: an unwrapped stick of gum, a colorful Rastafarian sweatband she'd sometimes worn on her left wrist, a cheap necklace with a Gothic cross, a black ceramic bowl she'd thrown perfectly on the wheel, and a plain white T-shirt that lay rumpled on the floor. I wanted to take that T-shirt and plug the hole in his heart, but having a few of Sarah's things and knowing she'd kept his letters—that started the healing process for him.

At the end of the week, when I came into his room, Christopher said he'd felt Sarah running across the soccer field beside him. He felt her next to him at the breakfast table and in his classroom and on the bus home from school.

Christopher's calm behavior had been a smokescreen for his feelings. I'd assumed he had handled Sarah's death better than the rest of us. I'd been very wrong. From that day on, I set aside one special night every week for the two of us.

In early November, I received a late-night call from the police telling me to pick up Caiti from a raucous party on the north end of the island. I was so angry I could barely see to drive. When I walked in the door, I silenced the proceedings with my rage, yelling at the kids to get a clue before somebody else got killed. I had never cursed so much in one mouthful. Even the police officers were taken aback. It didn't bother me one bit that Caiti was embarrassed. We sat in thunderous silence on the way home.

thanksgiving, year one

Our first Thanksgiving without Sarah, I prepared the usual meal—a twenty-two-pound turkey, homemade stuffing, steamed green beans, burnt-buttered garlic Brussels sprouts, creamed onions, mashed potatoes, sweet potato casserole, giblet gravy, Waldorf salad with mini marshmallows. For dessert, fresh pumpkin pie and apple pie with a slice of cheddar.

We recited grace together, then, following our tradition, each of us shared something for which we were thankful. That Thanksgiving was tough. Caiti was silent. Christopher mumbled. My mother's voice filled with tears. Andy maintained his restraint. I offered thanks for the family present at the table, and for the child whose reflection shimmered in the candlelight.

Caiti said her nightmares ended that Thanksgiving. Her dreams returned to normal, Sarah always included, as if she were alive.

There is much to be gained from the stability of ritual and tradition.

winter, year one

I find hope in the darkest of days,
And focus in the brightest.
I do not judge the universe.

—His Holiness, the Dalai Lama

December 7, 2004, Sarah's dad and grandmother met us at the courthouse. He'd flown in from Montana; she, from New York City. Every seat was filled with parents, friends, and the merely curious. The young driver, Hannah, flanked by her parents and her attorney, had already admitted her guilt and accepted the prosecution's charge— driving without a license and vehicular homicide. Hannah's father had chosen an attorney to represent his daughter's best interest but not to assert her innocence. I had much respect for that.

The swirl of noise ceased as the judge entered the courtroom. All eyes focused forward. About ten years older than I, I wondered if he had teenagers.

Judge Hartman invited testimony from our family. Sarah's dad spoke first: "She will always be my little girl. Time will not heal this wound. We live with the realization that we can search the world and not find Sarah anywhere."

Andy appealed for the parents and children of Bainbridge to learn from the tragedy. Caiti's words were bitter and angry. The father of the defendant responded, saying, "I know you don't believe me, Caiti, but I hope you will know at some point that Hannah is deeply sorry." Hannah spoke last, apologizing again to our family.

Finally, the judge addressed the hushed courtroom. "Responsibility for the crash rests not just on the driver's poor decision, but in part on all the teens in the car and their parents." Pausing to make eye contact around the courtroom, he continued, "If we deny this, we are deceiving ourselves."

Hannah was sentenced: fifteen to thirty-six weeks at a state juvenile prison, one hundred hours of community service, one year of probation, and financial restitution. State officials would determine the length of her incarceration.

How can anyone measure a just penalty for so much pain and suffering? And death.

My mother had no hesitation declaring that everyone involved should be held accountable. Accountable, accountable, accountable—the words like a scratched CD. Her granddaughter had been held account-able. She was dead. Accountable. The word ripped at my insides like a knife stabbing the same wound. Yes, I agreed, but *accountable* wasn't the word I would have chosen. I wasn't sure what word I would've chosen.

Besides being my main support, my mother focused her energies on the prosecution of the case. But her fierce words, spoken and writ-ten, depleted her health. Three days before the sentencing, she was hospitalized for a burst appendix.

She was just sixty-three, and this was a first hospital stay for her since her children were born. Caiti and Christopher needed her, and I needed her. I couldn't imagine my littlest children growing up with no Nonny. This couldn't be her time to die. I had to believe that Sarah wouldn't leave her alone in the hospital.

From her hospital bed, my mother prayed the rosary as we sat in the courtroom. After the sentencing, she made a rapid recovery. Mid-morning, December 10, I checked her out of the hospital. On the drive home, Mother said, "While you were in that courtroom, Sarah was with me." My eyes focused on the wet pavement as I braced for her story.

She described three different times, in and out of a dream that began with Mother and Sarah meeting in a small town, in the middle of Main Street, in the middle of nowhere. A blinding snowstorm had closed all the shops. Icicles hung from the eaves of the buildings; snow coated the branches of bare cherry trees lining the sidewalks. The town was silent and dead.

Wearing a sleeveless nightgown and a white rabbit cape over her shoulders, Mother carried a well-read book, on its cover, a Christmas wreath framing a photo of Sarah as a child.

The two walked along Main Street towards twilight, theirs the only footprints in the snow, everything quiet and magically still. A voice came out of the distance, saying, "Which way do you want to go? You can walk together toward the end of the street, or stay and enjoy the snowfall." Mother and Sarah stood absolutely still, like sculptures of ice. Mother said the dream continued after a second waking moment during the hospital emergency. The third awakening took her into the courtroom as the events unfolded.

Parked on the slope of Mother's driveway, I opened the door and helped her inside. I imagined Sarah, keeping watch at the hospital, grasping her grandmother's blue hospital gown, and willing her back to consciousness.

Now that Sarah was presumably keeping company with her grand-mother, I wondered if she would tease her about being a "clean freak." The first step Nonny took upon arriving home from the hospital was a beeline for the vacuum. Sometimes, the twins would giggle and say, "Nonny only poops pink powder puffs."

Though Mother had been teaching for twenty-five years as a read-ing specialist at a Catholic elementary school, I'd never seen her in the classroom. I knew her only as the loving person who took care of us, gave sage advice, and sustained us through hardships. However, as a woman independent of family life, I didn't know her at all. I decided to change that.

christmas, 2004

That holiday season was the first true test of how our family was doing. We'd made it through Thanksgiving by keeping to the usual tradition. But Christmas was more personal and nostalgic. I included Sarah's stocking on the mantle. We put up the tree and wrapped a few presents. On Christmas Eve, the family gathered at Jeff's house where Father Quigg said Mass.

The holidays remained constant.

Our first Christmas without Sarah, 2004

Six days later, we overheard talk of a large and joyous "Happy Fifteenth Birthday" celebration for the young driver convicted of killing Sarah. The next day she entered the juvenile detention center.

new year's day, 2005

> *We may encounter many defeats,*
> *But we must not be defeated.*
>
> —Maya Angelou

A deep breath reverberated through our home when we woke to New Year's Day 2005.

The new year brought with it the challenge to forgive. Forgiveness isn't something to be earned, and it doesn't come easily. But learning to forgive would lift the giant boulders of bitterness and free our hearts to heal. Of course, forgiving is different from forgetting, and we could never forget the accident, the events surrounding that day, and the aftermath. Those "not forgotten" blocks stack up with time, building thick walls. These "not forgotten" blocks are what I am left with. It's what I do with the "not forgetting," how I muddle through.

I wanted to understand the young driver as the immature child she was, making the same poor decision Sarah had made when she climbed into that car. Hannah's mother was herself a twin, so of course, she understood the powerful bond that had been broken when one of our twins was killed. Perhaps she would suffer more than her daughter. In spite of my efforts, the accident played over and over in my head. The driver expressed her apologies in a letter and in the courtroom. Her parents offered their apologies. Through the grapevine, I heard that she and her dad had flown to Montana to apologize to Sarah's dad. With apologies or without, I was hopeful that, given time, my family would find peace.

I heard somewhere that you can never get to the other side of a painful struggle without facing it head-on and going through it—not around, over, or under but through every hopeless, terrifying moment. If I had known what was ahead, I might have run away.

The second teenage driver had only one count: auto theft. Her court date was set for Wednesday, January 5, just before our family birthdays. Mary would be two on January 15; I would be forty-one on the twenty-first. Caiti's seventeenth birthday, the first in her life without Sarah, fell on February 5, quickly followed by my mother's on the eighth, just before Annie's first birthday on February 13.

On January 4, the phone rang.

A pleasant voice from Hall Health at the University of Washington was confirming an appointment for Sarah tomorrow at 10 a.m. She gave Sarah's birth date and home address.

Settling the lump obstructing my airway, I said in a faltering voice, "Sarah's not able to be there on Wednesday. She'll reschedule at another time." There had been no doctor's appointment scheduled for Sarah.

The floor came up and caught me as I sank in front of the kitchen sink. Actually I believed in ghosts. I believed in surges of electricity, remnants of light, and the continuum of energy. What did I think happened when someone died? Ashes to ashes, and dust to dust. Wasn't

Sarah with me when Grandmom told me about her aunt Josephine? I threw my hands over my mouth, crouched low on the tiled floor, and inhaled deeply.

the second hearing, january 5, 2005

Wednesday at 10 a.m., Judge Leila Mills presided over a packed, contentious courtroom. Hailey—the teenager who'd taken her parent's car—stood before the court. Her attorney arrived late. The parents were named as victims in the case and the charges pertained only to a stolen vehicle, not to vehicular homicide. When asked to address the judge, Hailey said, "I think I've been punished enough. It can't get any worse than this." Her statement shocked me. For our family, it was *much worse than this.*

Hailey was sentenced to the maximum penalty: twenty days in juvenile detention, twenty-four hours of community service, one year of probation, and restitution, counseling, and drug testing. Her lawyer requested a deferred disposition—meaning, if Hailey complied with all terms of her sentence, the case would be dismissed. The judge denied the request, saying that dismissing the charges for this minor would not benefit the community. The attorney said he and his client would go to trial. A recess was called to set a trial date, but by the time Judge Mills returned to the bench, the defendant pled guilty to second-degree auto theft, a felony conviction that could leave her with a criminal record for the rest of her life.

Faintly, I remember this fourteen-year-old in the courtroom. Vividly, I remember her attorney. Tall and lanky with designer glasses perched on a prominent nose, he seemed an actor on stage, arms flailing at his sides as he played out the scene.

Two days after the ruling, we distributed green wristbands, with the name "SARAH" on one side and the words, "Live 2 Love, Love 2

Live," on the other. This was a call to support and recognize the children of Bainbridge Island—reminding parents to cherish their children and asking teenagers to remember that one person's choices today can impact the lives of so many others—tomorrow and forever.

Donations collected from the distribution of the wristbands would fund the beginnings of a memorial garden, a place for students at the high school to gather when tragedy hit one of their own. One father whose teenager had died several years before, endorsed the project but said, "It's unlikely that few but you will remember your dead child as the years pass." His words crushed me.

Today, the garden lies fallow in a remote corner of the old gymnasium, filled with weeds.

february 5, 2005

> *To live in the hearts we leave behind is not to die.*
> —Thomas Campbell

On the fifth of February—Caiti and Sarah's seventeenth birthday—sheets of rain flooded the roads and filled the ditches. Andy volunteered to walk Lady before he left for work. Crossing back by the front garden, Lady suddenly bolted to Sarah's bedroom window, jumping into the dirt, furiously wagging her tail, and planting herself in front of the window, her head cocking to the left, then to the right, and back again, her tail thumping in the mud. Andy's instincts told him that something extraordinary was happening, but it was too much for him to process at the time. It would be two years before he told me the story.

This was the last year we sang "Happy Birthday" to Sarah.

Caiti and Sarah's sixth birthday party

Once we survived that first birthday season, I had a glimmer of hope that we might come out *okay*—eventually. The children gave me reason to wake up in the morning. Though one was missing, four still appeared at the breakfast table waiting to be fed. *Be strong for the littlest ones*, I thought. *We don't want them to be crippled by our sadness.*

Still, Andy and I never spoke of Sarah. We tended to our respective responsibilities like two people job-sharing on different shifts. We were locked in silence.

There were so many things to consider. In the first few months after the accident, it became clear that Caiti wouldn't graduate from high school unless she changed schools, but educational options on the island were limited. Halfway through her junior year, she enrolled at the alternative school on Bainbridge, which offered the flexibility she needed to complete her junior year of high school and continue through her senior year. Yes, she had isolated herself, but she was still alive and willing to try.

spring, year one

Spring 2005, with the cherry blossoms in full bloom, I caught the morning ferry and walked the mile uphill to the Social Security Office. Forty-five minutes later, a large woman in her late fifties called my number. She wore a cardigan sweater over a white blouse, her hair wrapped in a bun.

"I need to cancel this social security number," I said, handing her Sarah's birth certificate, death certificate, and social security card. She pulled up the number and typed in the date of death, then paused. Looking up, she met my wet eyes, "I'm so sorry. Was Sarah your daughter?" I nodded. "I'll keep your family in my prayers," she said.

"Thank you," I mouthed the words. The walk back to the ferry terminal seemed like too many miles.

That spring, Andy and I visited an estate attorney. I dragged Caiti with us, insisting she put her thoughts to paper, to keep things simple for me, just in case. Another item checked off the to-do list.

For Christmas 2005, Andy gave me my first computer. It was bright and shiny in comparison to the old wooden secretary desk inherited from Andy's mother. I taped a small photo of Sarah to the monitor.

Technology was a slow learning curve for me, a foreign language. So while my little girls played on a blanket, I worked through the learning curve. I was reminded of Caiti and Sarah playing around me as I worked on the sewing machine in those long-ago days, between naps and errands and dinner.

One day in March, I turned off the computer and lay on the floor with Mary and Annie and Lady. After a cold and drizzly day, the sun broke through and beamed into the room, warming Lady's belly. But within moments, she jumped to her feet, and stood at attention as the printer churned to life. Annie turned her head to the noise. Mary toddled towards the sound. As I approached the old secretary, a single sheet of paper emerged. Printed in all capitals, the letters spelled:

F L O W E R B L A C K

Sarah's energy filled the alcove, the warmth embracing and surrounding me. Lady and the girls were quiet, almost expectant. I read and reread each letter, passing my sleeve across my eyes to wipe the tears away. Quietly, delicately, I nestled the paper in the top drawer of my closet. What are miracles except occurrences we don't understand?

Please, when death comes into my world, don't tell me I must get over it. "Get over it" is not the right choice of words. Death is something I am learning to move through. I am learning to weave it into my daily life. I will never get over Sarah's death.

Though Mary and Annie would never know Sarah's touch, how she danced or the sound of her voice, her memory remained alive in our home. I wove her name into daily conversation with stories and laughter. Repeating her name made death easier to digest. Each night, we lit Sarah's candle honoring her presence in our family, reciting bedtime prayers for her soul, her guidance, and her help.

In public, I played a game of truthful omission: I claimed five children; Sarah was in Seattle; Caiti was a junior in high school; Christopher was starting middle school; Mary and Annie, toddlers. By not saying that Sarah *was living* in Seattle, I diverted the conversation.

In spring, Sarah loved to set her easel and canvas against an old tree trunk so she could paint the cherry trees in our orchard. Sometimes she sketched; sometimes she painted. Though there were only seven trees in the orchard, each one was a different variety, a different size, all blooming in a profusion of pink.

One painting showed the whole tree in blossom; in another, just a single blossom filled the eighteen-inch-square canvas; yet in another, a branch was bursting with blossoms and buds. Each year offered a pictorial of Sarah's growth and maturity as an artist. In spring, her paintings decorated the kitchen and dining nook. Once the blossoms outside were spent, the paintings inside were put away till the following spring. Painted cherry trees.

But in 2005, when Sarah's paintings came down, Caiti was disconsolate and began a campaign to leave the island and stay with a friend's family on Maui, assuring me that her classes and schoolwork could be completed on the Internet. Bainbridge was like a repetitive hand of losing cards for her. Sadly watching her pack her pink duffle bag, I thought, "This must be how it feels to lose the other half of yourself." Caiti was seventeen years old and desperately lost, and I must have been desperately confused, dropping her curbside at the Seattle-Tacoma airport, with a one-way ticket.

exploring the other side

> *Perhaps they are not stars,*
> *but rather openings in heaven*
> *where the love of our lost ones pours through*
> *and shines down upon us*
> *to let us know they are happy.*
>
> —Eskimo Proverb

Three days later, I boarded a flight to Maui. This wasn't a time for Caiti to live among compassionate strangers; it was a time when we most needed to be together.

I wasn't too surprised when Caiti asked to visit a psychic. We had already felt glimmers of Sarah's presence. And we were both open to exploring other dimensions. Most of all, if it helped Caiti, I was all for it.

After asking around for a day or so, we found ourselves in a small surfing village called Paia, gazing at a bulletin board covered with messages, ads, people offering services, people looking for services, items for sale—a flea market with thumb tacks. And then, a tiny, jagged scrap of yellowed paper, scribbled with the message, "Stewart, Psychic Reader." Caiti begged me to call.

Dialing ... waiting ... waiting ... waiting ... finally he answered. Giving no details, I asked, "Would you have time today to talk with my daughter?" Caiti fidgeted in her flip-flops. We were taking an early flight home on Monday morning.

To my disappointment, Stewart responded, "It's Sunday. I don't work on Sundays. Can we meet on Monday?" Before I could plead our case, he said, "Please hold the line for a minute. My teakettle is singing." Less than a minute later, he agreed to meet us at 11:00 a.m.

Jittery and excited, we parked the Jeep in the last available space and watched as a stranger got out of a dumpy gray sedan and walked in our direction. He was tall and tan, with silver hair flowing down his back.

After the introductions, Stewart began to speak of a young girl with a dog beside her, telling us that when he had left the phone to tend the teakettle, she had yanked at his arm, urging him to meet us, the dog's tail swooshing the tiled floor. He smiled as he said, "I couldn't refuse that girl. She had a beaming smile with eyes as bright as the clear water. So, here I am."

Giving Caiti a hug, I stayed behind as the two of them strolled toward the beach. I prayed that this man's message would bring some relief for Caiti, that his powers were real. Almost two hours later, she climbed back into the Jeep.

"Mom. I believe it was Sarah and Emmett that Stewart saw in his kitchen. He knew Sarah was my twin. He knew how she was killed, even that the back of her head was crushed in the accident. He described Emmett as a huge chocolate lab. I didn't feed him any information. I never even told him I was a twin or that my twin was dead. I only told him my name."

To say the least, I clung to every word. Caiti continued. "He told me Sarah chose to go to the other side, that it was her decision, that Sarah knew the two of us could work better together with me on this side and her on the other, that she'd help me dream bigger and make those dreams happen." I wondered if Stewart knew they were mirror-image twins. I wondered if that was what he meant when he said my twins could work better apart, facing each other from opposite sides of a mirror.

Caiti paused, gazing out at the ocean. "Stewart told me Sarah didn't feel any pain when she died. It didn't hurt her. It just happened."

Ragtop down, we drove to the top of Haleakala. Ten thousand feet above the ocean, barren, views seeming endless like swells coming off the horizon. The wind captured our voices as we walked the trail to the observatory. If I had asked any questions, Caiti wouldn't have heard me.

Two years later, on a family vacation to Maui, I returned to that bulletin board and searched for Stewart's name and number. I found nothing. I inquired at the grocery store and asked a few locals who hung out at the corner coffee shop. Everyone claimed to know him, but nobody could say where he'd gone.

While Caiti and I were in Hawaii, my granddad (my mother's father) died. His death from Alzheimer's was expected, and even a relief. At last, he was set free from a terrible disease from which there was no return. Why death had to be so cruel made no sense to me. My family gathered for another funeral. Two weeks later, my mother suffered a mild heart attack. The fear of more loss was overwhelming.

Before summer began, lawsuits were filed: two complaints; eight different parties; varying degrees of injuries, and one death. Both of the drivers' families sold their homes and moved to other cities. In our community, the shock and dismay continued in our community.

summer, year one

Nearly a year after the accident, we put the house on the market.

Each time I opened the front door, I revisited that August morning—two tired men, burdened with terrible news, asking if I was Sarah's mother. Looking out over the front yard took me back to Sarah's party where so many people had celebrated her life. If we were ever going to heal as a family, we had to move from this house. Andy made a DVD outlining the features of the property and put a sales package together. Within six weeks, we had a solid offer—much sooner than we'd expected.

Andy set the closing date for August 23—the anniversary of Sarah's death. He saw it as closure. I saw it as disregard.

We decided to buy another piece of property and build again. Andy and I were good at building. That is—we could build anything except an open line of communication. I hoped that creating a new home would give us a shared sense of cooperation and purpose.

With only a month to pack up and move, I attacked each room, sorting and discarding in preparation for the new chapter in our lives. Sarah's bedroom I saved for last, allowing myself all the time I needed to slowly, carefully, sort through her things. I needed the silence of the house, just my dog with me, enough time with no interference.

I set aside a full day while my mother cared for Mary and Annie and Christopher stayed with a friend. Andy left for a short getaway to Hood River. Caiti slept in her room.

Nobody asked any questions. Everyone understood that packing away Sarah's bedroom would permanently erase her private space. The altar I'd created for her remained on the windowsill where we lit a candle for her every night. And my closet still held the sanctuary where I could close myself away when the tears wouldn't stop.

I could erase Sarah's space but I could never erase the stretch marks on my stomach. Looking in the mirror each morning, I am always reminded I have twins. Just as giving birth to twins had never crossed my mind, having a child die had never crossed my mind.

the painted trunk

For their twelfth Christmas, I painted a trunk for each of the twins with positive affirmations around the lids. Sarah's read: *See yourself moving through the day with a smile on your face and joy in your heart. Always have something to look forward to.* Another read, *Life is a great big canvas and you should throw all the paint on it you can.* My divorce had been finalized only a year before that Christmas. Positive affirmations were very important to me then. Now just four years later, Sarah would never see another Christmas, and I would pack her trunk one last time.

Early morning sun streamed through the windows, casting a perfect beam on Lady, stretched out and lying belly up on Sarah's rug. Deliberately, I placed a hand at each end of the trunk lid and pulled it open like a treasure chest, surprised to find it empty. Into the trunk, I began packing Sarah's yearbooks from middle school through sophomore year, all stuffed with quirky quotes, friends' autographs, and scribbled notations.

I added a paperback of *The Chosen,* a favorite of hers. The story speaks to the strength of friendship, the pursuit of truth, and making your own choices instead of following the life expected of you. In Chapter Four, the father tells his son to "choose a teacher and choose a friend." Roald Dahl was another favorite author. I packed Sarah's collection of his books.

From her desk, I pulled out the stack of letters from Christopher. Among the letters and scattered photos of Caiti and friends was Sarah's essay—her final English assignment. All of these things—the letters, photos, her essay, and other scraps of paper preserving her handwriting—I carefully placed in her trunk.

I protected her perfume bottles with bubble wrap and placed them back in their tray, added a few favorite stuffed animals—including the ninja turtle her friend had won for her at the county fair; the worn, stuffed, black lab puppy Santa had brought when she was three; the now tattered and faded yellow swatch of the baby blanket she clutched every night; her wood-handled hairbrush, bristles still wound with strands of dyed chocolate-brown hair; a favorite pair of black patent-leather high heels and a well-worn pair of Nike tennis shoes; an MP3 player with all her favorite music; her very first canvas painted in the orchard behind our Bainbridge firehouse; her gold baptismal cross and plastic glow-in-the-dark rosary; the jewelry box filled with baby teeth she'd bartered with the tooth fairy, plus her accompanying notes; a few pottery pieces she'd spun on the wheel, some lopsided because she struggled to center the slab, and a few pieces she'd sculpted by hand, in particular, the green ceramic piggy bank molded after the likes of Harry Potter; her poetry journal—chosen words delicately written in her left slant;

her gypsy ring from summer camp; the eyeglass pouch she'd knitted while I knitted a sweater; her first pair of white leather shoes, scuffed; her series of watercolors mimicking Picasso; the two-foot trophy from the City of Seattle for academic and sports excellence, awarded when she was nine; her contract, soundtrack, and autographed playbill from the musical production of *Showboat* (she had played the granddaughter, at age eight, with her Broadway-star grandma, Anita Gillette, at the Paramount Theatre); another favorite shirt stuffed under her bed; her light pink strapless chiffon dress from eighth-grade graduation ceremonies; her red silk dress from the spring tolo dance; her favorite red lace bra crumpled in the bottom of her jeans drawer; and the few pieces of costume jewelry she wore. These treasures were placed in her trunk, each connecting us and keeping Sarah in the heart of our family.

Before closing the lid, I placed inside a folder containing her obituary, the death certificate, and the toxicology report; a sealed envelope with the pierced jewelry removed from her body; a copy of the booklet and photo each guest had received at her celebration; her social security card, now stamped and invalidated; and copies of her birth and baptismal certificates. Finally, I added the red wallet containing her school ID card, driver's permit, and a few dollars and then a Ziploc bag containing her baby book and the ID tags she'd worn on her left wrist and right ankle when she arrived home from the hospital, just five days old. The twins wore those tags for a month.

Sarah's lambskin rug would always be beside my bed: each night, a reminder of the child who no longer lived with me, but *within* me now. Each morning, my feet would land where Sarah's had begun each day.

Morning hours turned to early afternoon before each item had been lovingly sorted and packed. Three moving boxes held reusable clothing, books, gadgets, and items with no personal value. I stuffed two large green trash bags with bedding and items to be discarded. I placed her shoes in a separate storage box; I couldn't part with them. Finally, her bedroom stripped bare, the sense of finality at the gravesite washed over me again, bringing me to my knees. Nothing would ever be the same.

Since that day, though I have opened the lid only a few times—to add a few mementoes from the anniversaries of her death or toss in a handful of cards from those who have sent remembrances—Sarah's trunk remains one of my most cherished treasures.

Sarah's trunk

august 23, 2005

It is only with the heart that one can see rightly;
What is essential is invisible to the eye.

—Antoine de Saint-Exupéry

*A*nd so, as Andy had scheduled it, the sale of our house closed on the first anniversary of Sarah's death while I had invited family and friends to honor her at the cemetery for a brief service and a meal at one of her favorite restaurants, Buca di Beppo. While Andy made one last inspection of the house in preparation for the closing, I would get the family ready. We agreed to take two cars.

Driving the long, gravel driveway, Andy parked his dusty Dodge Ram on the cobblestones. Morning sun filtered through the arms of giant cedars and hemlocks, curving through the branches of old maples. Dew glistened on the needles of the tall evergreens. Fading in the distance was a memory of Caiti and Sarah's old blue Jeep, parked to the side of the garage, where patches of oil still blotched the dirt.

While he toured the property, assuring himself that everything was ready for the new owners, I was driving to the ferry dock with Caiti and Christopher, fighting back a surge of anger. This was Sarah's day. We needed to be together as a family.

At 9:45, certain that the house was in order, Andy got back into his truck, prepared to make the 10:20 ferry. But ... the car keys were missing from his pocket. He scrambled, retracing his steps around the house, searching inside and around the truck. No keys. Anxious and confused, he returned to the front porch and slumped onto the bottom step. The ferry left without him.

He spotted a Mason jar filled with wild sweet peas and stacks of lupine in purples and bright pinks. Underneath was a note on a small scrap of paper. Collecting himself, he grabbed the flowers and the note and dashed back to the truck. In one motion, he crammed the jar into a cup holder, jammed the note into the side, grabbed his phone, and called my cell.

I was not pleased. Andy had failed Sarah and disappointed me. There was nothing more to say. Caiti, Christopher, and I drove to Calvary, alone.

Sitting in the truck, Andy heard the singing of frogs under thick, dark leaves in the shade of the garden beds, breaking the silence surrounding our old house. Taking notice of the flowers next to his water bottle, he began reading the scribbled note. It had but two lines, one an assurance to Sarah's family that she would not be forgotten; on the next, the three boys had signed their names.

As tears rolled down his cheeks and he returned the scrap of paper to the cup holder, his fingers touched the keys. He simply hadn't seen them before. He poured some water into the Mason jar.

Andy made the next boat. Though he would be late to the cemetery, everyone waited. We were in no rush. This day, Sarah's day, Andy arrived for his family, greeting us with a warm and heartfelt embrace. He pulled Christopher in, holding the two of us for a long time, then turned to Caiti, placing his two hands on her delicate shoulders and pulling her head against his chest. The August sun stretched across our family plot, the grassy knoll freshly mown. It had been a long year—taking one day at a time, then one week at a time, then one month at a time, until finally, the first year had passed. We were still a family, after all.

We were grateful for our friends and family that day, those who had supported us with so much concern and kindness, including a handful of Caiti and Sarah's friends.

One guest was a retired carpenter, named Robert—a Vietnam vet—who did the finishing work on our house. A man of very few words, Robert worked on his own schedule and honored Sarah's memory by handcrafting a plain wooden cross to mark the crash site on Tolo Road.

Suspecting that many years might pass before I had the courage to see his work, Robert brought the structure to our house before installing it. Towering more than six feet, it was grooved by hand with five capitalized letters across the horizontal beam, S A R A H. I traced each letter of Sarah's name, and then slid the palm of my left hand over the words, *Age 16 August 23, 2004,* engraved down the vertical timber. He placed it on Tolo Road at the site of the accident. Whether or not I could ever bear to drive that road where my daughter died, I was appreciative that she would be memorialized there—a wooden cross on the side of the road.

Sarah's wooden cross on Tolo Road

Several months after the accident, I noted a wooden cross at the intersection of Bucklin Hill and Fletcher Bay Roads. Blending into the trees, and silvered with the passage of time, the cross read: ANNIE MAE, KILLED 9-12-1985. I had never noticed the cross until after Sarah died, even though I passed it every day. Someone's child died here. I wondered if it was the first day of school, if she was riding her bike or walking. Every time I passed Annie Mae's wooden cross, my heart ached.

Six years later, after sharing the story of Annie Mae's wooden cross with a longtime resident of the island and reporting that her cross has suddenly vanished, the islander tells me that Annie Mae was a cow, killed at that intersection, the cross standing guard for twenty-five years. When I realize that so many prayers, intended for a dead child and a dead child's family have been sent up for a cow and her loving owner, the news gives me a good laugh. As it turns out, Annie Mae's owner has only recently passed away at age ninety. Prayers are never wasted.

The vice principal of Bainbridge High School—Ben Harper—was another honored guest at the anniversary service, marking the beginning of this second year. He mentioned Sarah's bright smile, random remarks, laughter, and lively conversation, adding that she often brought a new dimension to his day.

On one of those "new dimension" days, she was called into his office. Apparently, Caiti had had a problem with a schoolmate, and Sarah took matters into her own hands, saying, "Keep your distance from my twin sister, or I'm gonna kick your butt." The vice principal shook his head in mock exasperation and smiled, as Sarah giggled. He sent her back to class, watching as she sauntered the hallways with a carefree stride. Yep, he was describing the right twin.

Connor, Sarah's good friend, whose leg was now restored after several surgeries and a year of physical therapy, arrived with his mother and brought a small bouquet of white roses. Here, at Calvary, with one mother standing beside her son, I was the other mother, the one whose child lay buried in this hallowed ground. Standing together that day in remembrance of Sarah, sharing our grief and support, our lives would be forever connected.

Another guest, Sal, was one of the volunteer firefighters that August night, helping the crews who tore the car open, moving around Sarah's lifeless body as she lay beside the wreckage. Before the white sheet was laid over her still body, he placed her slender arms over her heart, leaving her in peaceful sleep. Before this first anniversary, I didn't know him.

Today, a connection exists between Sal and our family that can't be explained.

While forty of us gathered at the gravesite that day, Father Quigg offered a few prayers and evoked a few laughs. Caiti, again, leaned against the L'Abbe monument, again distancing herself from the group, standing off to the side without lifting her head or joining in the singing or sharing a memory, the black mascara defining her swollen eyes smudged across the pale whites of her cheeks. I wondered if she had visited the cemetery since the funeral. Had she ever looked at her sister's name engraved in the granite cap? Or run her fingers across the letters? Though my heart broke for her, I felt powerless to ease her pain.

Christopher stood at my right side, singing "Amazing Grace" and "The Circle Game," a few tears on his cheeks. The year had aged him, not only in growing taller but also in giving him a seriousness and thoughtfulness beyond his years.

Andy and I joined hands and hearts that day. There was a change in him—a strength in his grip, an understanding that today was different from yesterday. Neither of us knew what tomorrow would bring, but today, we stood strong.

I closed the observance with a letter to Sarah:

Sweet Child,

You always loved a good party. I miss you.

It's been a very long year for me. But I am finally under-standing and accepting that your death is your greatest gift to me, to each of us. Strange as it sounds ... but, yes, with this gift, I am learning to live with more patience, more compassion, more kindness, more giving, and more grace. My bonds with family and friends are strengthening. I understand now we are each a gift to one another. My husband, each of my children, and you have been gifted to me for only a short time, and we know now that these gifts can be taken from us at any time. We have today. We have now together. It is with my faith that I journey through each day. And God knows, it is only with this greatest gift of all from you my faith continues to grow. For I know for certain, I will be with you again. I know your spirit is with us now. I hold tight to my memories. And so, I thank you. Thank you, my child, for the years shared with me, for all your gifts to me. I love you so very much.

Mom

Death is not extinguishing the light.
It is putting out the lamp because dawn has come.
—Rabindranath Tagore

Every mother wants to know that her child is remembered here on earth and has come to peace somewhere beyond. Surely when Sarah reached the other side of here and now, she became aware of everything true: the joy a smile can bring, the power hidden in the obvious, the importance of living today, the significance of investing yourself in family, the priceless gift of friendship. I'm sure she knew that possessions didn't give life substance, that family wasn't limited to the traditional sense but included many—the extended family who sparked her flame, the friends who shared the daily moments, and the strangers who filled in all the gaps. Wherever she is now, I believe Sarah knows the truth.

And so, we continued on.

 *year two*

*A mother's love for her child
is like nothing else in the world.
It knows no law, no pity, it dates all things
and crushes down remorselessly all that stands in its path.*

—Agatha Christie

Caiti celebrated her eighteenth birthday. Christopher entered a small middle school with mostly unfamiliar faces. Mary turned three in January; Annie, two in February. With hesitation, I spoke more openly about Sarah's death. Andy had glimpses of his own buried conflicts but was not yet ready to confront them. My mother stayed the course, continuing to care for her own mother.

During the second year, my mother's sister, Aunt Lindy, gave generously of her time and wisdom. Living a thousand miles away in California, she had an inspired sense of timing during that trying year, somehow sensing the moments when I most needed an empathetic ear to listen or an understanding voice to fill the void. She seemed to understand that the universe could misplace *its* sense of order, could disrupt *our* sense of order. I wondered if there was order to the universe or if God left us all in a state of chaos on the sixth day before He rested. She is a constant reminder that wisdom and patience are the gifts of age and experience.

fall, year two

Caiti remained closed emotionally and physically. On rare occasions, when she joined us at the dinner table, she sat aimlessly pushing her food around the plate as if searching for a lost earring. Friends gradually drifted away. She medicated herself with sleep, taking sleeping pills to hide herself in a gauzy half-life where she could be with Sarah in their world, where nothing had changed, where they were still "The Twins."

When she couldn't sleep, Caiti took the car out and drove the dark and peaceful island roads, listening to her music, calming her anxieties, and passing time. I couldn't bring myself to take away the car keys. Driving was her only release besides sleeping. But, several weeks after Sarah's first anniversary, Caiti ran the car into a ditch. Leaving the car and her cell phone behind, she walked away without a scratch and crawled into bed at a friend's house. When I heard another early-morning knock, my heart stopped. The police officer reported the wreck, but Caiti was not in the car.

Surfacing later that morning, Caiti apologized. I was devastated. When I'd bought Sarah's plot at Calvary, I bought the right to bury two people. That was how the cemetery sold plots. To me, it was only logical that the twins—Sarah sharing her lifetime with Caiti—would be buried together, boxes of ashes stacked in the same grave. Strange as it seemed, it was a daily thought that comforted me. But now, this was the wake-up call to stop hoping that things would improve and for me to take decisive action.

Though reluctant, Caiti committed to a yearlong therapy regimen that included group therapy and individual counseling. Every Tuesday afternoon, she met with a therapist for an hour, after which we would have dinner at a nearby restaurant and return for a two-hour group session. Six months later, we quit.

During my desperate struggle to help Caiti, a friend suggested volunteer work at Helpline House—a community outreach program that helps islanders in need. The friend quoted Viktor Frankl, a Holocaust survivor: "When all seems helpless, help someone else."

Caiti had no interest in volunteering or anything else, but she was convinced that she wanted to leave Bainbridge, and college was the answer. I assured her that volunteer work would look good on a college application. To sweeten the pot even more, I offered to pay fair wages for every hour that she volunteered. Teenagers always need money.

While the new house was under construction, we lived in a rental. It was cold and bare with old, single-pane windows rattling with the chilled winds off Puget Sound.

One Tuesday evening in late October, Caiti and I returned from Seattle to find Christopher and the sitter huddled in the kitchen, both visibly upset. Andy was out with friends. Our sitter, Janelle, described putting the little girls to bed, saying goodnight to Christopher who was in his room watching TV, and lying down to doze in Annie's extra bed. A little later, she was startled awake by what she thought were footsteps in the hall and the sound of a voice calling "Mom," growing louder as the voice neared Annie's bedroom. Jumping into the hallway, she came face-to-face with a very shaken Christopher, who was sure he had heard Sarah calling my name.

"Don't worry," I told them. "I hear her, too." We couldn't possibly explain what was happening, but somehow, we knew Sarah was there with us.

A few weeks later, very early in the morning, as I was brewing coffee, Caiti appeared in the kitchen. She described a visit from Sarah in her dreams.

"Sarah said she didn't feel any pain when she was killed. Her world, it's like ours. She likes it there." Caiti became quiet, then and drank a glass of milk before going back to bed. I poured a second cup of coffee and added cream. Until that moment, I had not known that Caiti was terrified that her sister had suffered when she was killed, and suffered still.

We planted a memorial garden for Sarah at the cemetery. The previous April on an early morning walk, I had come upon a tree covered with blazing blossoms that mimicked the colors of Sarah's paintings. The branches stretched fifteen feet from a trunk at least twelve inches in diameter. On the metal plaque at its base was the name: Prairiefire Flowering Crabapple.

A wide circular hole was dug to fit the diameter of the bur-lapped root ball of our Prairiefire—the largest trunk available, two and a half inches, special ordered from Bainbridge Gardens. A metal plaque engraved, "Sarah's Garden," along with the botanical name of the tree, was placed next to the trunk.

The description said that the tree would grow slowly. That was okay. Sarah would be there a long time. And I had time to wait. Years from now, the Prairiefire would offer shade from the summer sun, and I'd be able to visit my child, sheltered beneath the colorful blossoms, gazing over Lake Washington, all the way to Mount Rainier, marking the passing years. Papa Ed, Sarah's grandfather, volunteered to tend to her garden. To him, she had been an angel.

Each year, Papa Ed plants bright pink geraniums in late spring, purple and white winter pansies in late fall. Bulbs—tulips and daffodils—fill in, between February and April. Every two weeks, he weeds, plucks the spent flowers, and trims the grass. Slowly he widens the square, inch by inch with the flat blade of his hoe. More space is needed for more flowers. Sarah's uncle, Geordie, has placed a slender white crystal, about seven inches tall, against the base of the tree.

Sporadically, over the months and years, more plants, cut flowers, and ornaments adorn Sarah's tree. When I arrive to find these loving gifts, I am awakened.

winter, year two

With the second birthday season, Sarah's name was not included in the birthday song. On February 5, I went alone to the cemetery, taking pink Gerbera daisies. Afterward, I picked up Caiti so we could spend the day together. Keeping busy on the birthday was best for both of us. From now on, it would be Caiti's day, celebrating my daughter who celebrates another year.

But Sarah's anniversaries I embrace. That August day is also a day of celebration, a day to recognize that Sarah has journeyed onward and we, as a family, have grown stronger. Maneuvering through January and February with all those birthdays is a victory lap for the power of love and the conviction that life is always worth living.

One February evening, after tucking everyone in, I went back to Annie's room to get my magazine. Opening the bedroom door, my eyes deceivingly caught Sarah asleep in the double bed—tucked in for the night, the bed sheets pulled up under her chin, knees wrapped towards her chest—her outline exactly as I remembered. In my mind's eye, there they were, my smallest child asleep in the crib next to Sarah. It was just past ten o'clock.

I stood in the doorway listening to Annie's short breaths and catching my own as the covers rose and fell in the double bed. I was calm and awake. Sarah's skin was clear and healthy, lips plump, hair shining silky-chocolate, natural soft waves splayed across the top sheet. Gazing into the quiet room, memory carried me back to another time, when I was a young mother and Sarah was Annie's age ... to the top floor of our walkup apartment on Queen Anne Hill ... to restless nights with two young twin girls ... to bathtub smiles and birthmarks ... to blond curls. Memories so vivid, I could have touched them, like gently taking a child's hand. I took a deep breath and let my heart expand with love and peace.

Caiti and Sarah, 8 months old

spring, year two

The cherry blossoms came early that year. I hung Sarah's paintings in our temporary kitchen, pounding new nail holes, larger than at our old house. I wanted to leave Sarah's mark.

Grandmom's ninetieth birthday, March 2006

This spring marked Grandmom's ninetieth birthday. Her five children, twelve grandchildren, and ten great-grandchildren gathered to celebrate in a private room on the fifteenth floor of her retirement home, where toasts were offered up and a meal shared. Of course, I included Sarah in the count.

> *Don't be afraid to cry.*
> *It will free your mind of sorrowful thoughts.*
>
> —Hopi saying

In April 2006, Kitsap County Health announced a free class on grieving, open to anyone eighteen years or older.

Caiti, now just eighteen, was the youngest among twenty adults in that first meeting. A circle of metal chairs filled the plain meeting room, where we sat across from the two hospice facilitators. Two more people stood in the rear.

I was extremely reluctant to express my grief openly in a group. Until now, I'd held myself in check, trying to appear strong and in control, trying to assure my children everything would be okay, trying to assure myself, as well.

This stoicism had not helped Caiti at all. She was still living in her own world: numb, sleepy, and lethargic. The volunteer work at Helpline House had helped somewhat. She had completed enough classes to graduate from high school with acceptance letters from the colleges to which she'd applied. My hope for this grief counseling was that Caiti would open up and embrace her life again, knowing that all had not died with Sarah, that she was not alone.

When the hospice director invited us to introduce ourselves, Caiti seemed thousands of miles away, slumped in the metal chair, eyes fixed on her pink-painted toes, the frayed hems of her pink sweatpants dragging over her flip-flops.

As we went around the circle, everyone had a story to tell about loss and grief, each individual echoing the next. The second to speak was the oldest man in the group, married for more than sixty-two years. "I miss my wife," he said, as if he cradled her heart in his palm. He and his wife had lived together for more time than either Caiti or I could know. Another man, about my age, awoke one morning to find his wife had passed during the night—an unexpected death. Two teenage daughters asleep upstairs, it was a school day. Then there was a woman, who lived alone with her four cats, still grieving the loss of her mother after fourteen years.

When the circle of introductions came around to Caiti, I nervously lowered my head and closed my eyes. "I'm Caiti. My twin sister was killed in a car crash in August 2004. I miss her and just want her to come home." Without tears she continued, "I know she's not coming home. But I wish she were. I'm having a hard time living without her." Then it was my turn. Caiti's clarity washed away my strength like a strong undercurrent. But if Caiti had been brave enough, I couldn't retreat.

"I'm Caroline, Caiti's mom." A lump blocked my throat. Caiti wrapped her arm around my shoulder. That was all I could say. My child saw her mother broken, and she comforted me.

We found freedom that night in an unexpected place with a group of kind and understanding strangers who knew the landscape of death as well as we did. Death was no longer an experience locked inside us. We drove home in silence, recognizing that something profound had changed in our lives.

For the next ten weeks, Caiti and I listened far more than we contributed. But now, we knew we were not alone.

summer, year two

At last, the Class of 2006 graduated from Bainbridge High School, almost two years after the accident. A lifetime for Sarah. Most of the gossip had finally died down.

I sat in the back, hiding behind sunglasses, as Caiti walked the stage to receive her diploma, wearing cap and gown, adorned by a purple lei. The word was out that the teachers and administrators were greatly relieved to see this group graduate. They were weary of the sniping, blame, and group warfare, and though the hostility had eased, it had never completely stopped.

But today, the Class of 2006 was moving on—young people off to college and bright futures—the troubles of the past left behind that sunny day. I was glad for them, and happier still for Caiti. But, not to see Sarah walk across that stage ...

High school graduation, June 2006

Finally, I felt ready to focus on my own grief and healing. An acquaintance recommended a therapist who had been very helpful to her. I had nothing to lose and no expectations.

Entering Patricia's office, I was startled to see a square tub chair, upholstered in a beige-patterned silk. It was identical to a chair in our living room—the same chair, same fabric, same tattered threads. (We had inherited ours from Andy's mother.) Spiritual books and artifacts from around the world lined the walls of the office. A small candle flickered on the coffee table. Though I'd not met her before, Patricia seemed very familiar to me. She had grown up in the same Seattle neighborhood as my mother's family. A few years younger than Aunt Lindy, she had shoulder-length silver hair and wore black leggings under a tunic, her wrists wrapped in bracelets, no wedding band. Her hands had known work. Her movements were steady and slow, her voice calm and comfortable. The space here was serene and safe, a place where I could begin to release the pain and grief I'd held in for so long. It was more exhausting than I could ever have imagined, yet I felt willing to give my whole self to it.

Patricia challenged me to look at things from other perspectives. Telling stories of spiritual beliefs and rituals from around the world, she helped me to understand that tragedy in life is inevitable, that it can't always be avoided. She also confirmed that, in the face of blinding sorrow, kindness seems to be universal. Compassion lives. In the aftermath, gifts can be found, some deeply profound, no matter what faith you live or what you believe. Every moment I sat in that familiar chair—in that warm, safe place—was a motion forward, one step at a time.

year three

*Within you there is a stillness and a sanctuary to which you can
retreat at any time and be yourself, just as I can.*

—Hermann Hesse

W hat had happened, happened. There was nothing anyone could
do to change the outcome of that August night in 2004. We had
gradually settled into a new reality. I had to stop looking for the whys
and wherefores that could never be explained.

The story of the "terrible accident on Tolo Road" evokes memories
and conversation, even today, years later. During those times, it brought
Sarah's death and Caiti's suffering immediately to mind. Whoever
knew Sarah's story, knew Caiti's story. Sometimes, people slipped up
and called Caiti by Sarah's name. Though she smiled and waved their
embarrassment away, her heart twisted and her stomach wrenched.
She was brave. How difficult that must have been.

I was culpable, too, often searching for Sarah in Caiti's blue eyes.
I'm sure Caiti must have known that.

Two days before Sarah's second anniversary, on August 21, 2006,
we packed Caiti's car, and she drove across the Tacoma Narrows Bridge
to attend University of Puget Sound—one hour and fifteen minutes
from home.

As Caiti left Bainbridge Island behind, crossing over the Agate
Pass Bridge, blasting her favorite music, and singing along with Tupac

and Billy Joel—"Only the Good Die Young"—armloads of sad memories fell to the wayside. Regrets were fading, fatigue vanishing. When one of Sarah's favorite songs—"What A Wonderful World" by Louis Armstrong—played on her iPod, Caiti sang along. I was immeasurably proud of her courage, proud of her for making it through.

In my car, I followed Caiti across the bridge and down the highway with Mary and Annie strapped in their car seats. Laurie Berkner's children music—"I'm Gonna Catch You"—played on the stereo.

fall, year three

With Caiti away at school, there was more space for me. Though the phone rang often while Caiti adjusted to college life and the separation was hard for both of us, I knew she could, and must, find her own way.

Four weeks after she started school, Caiti wanted to come home. She was fragile and insecure, desperately missing Sarah's strength and confidence. I worried that if she left college now and returned home, she might never be strong enough to leave again.

That night, after the children were asleep, I broke down and reached out to Andy. In despair, I questioned everything, including my faith. After letting me pour it all out, with a quiet strength, he held me. After I calmed down, together we peeked in on Christopher and then checked on Mary and Annie, certain they were safe—pale blue fleece blankets pulled up, arms and feet tucked in.

The next morning, we found the girls wrapped in their sleeping bags instead of their fleece blankets. Kept in baskets under their cribs, the bags were used when we traveled. Still asleep at 7:30 in the morning, the girls were warm and content. Breathing. Things happened I could not explain. Gradually, I was learning to let go and let things be.

The time had come to shift my attention to Christopher, Mary, and Annie. I'd done my best to give them what they needed. But two years of my own pain and Caiti's intense grief had sapped my physical and emotional energy. Mary started preschool in the fall of year three, giving me a few hours alone with Annie, our youngest. Finally, I could go to Christopher's games and stay the whole time. There was more space in my life. I could think and see more clearly than ever before.

Annie, who was just finding her words, would point to the first star and say Sarah's name. She looked at photos of Caiti and Sarah and knew them apart. Sometimes she wrapped her arms around her chest, hugging herself, calling it a hug from Sarah.

Christopher was becoming his own man—strong, but sensitive in ways that even most grown men may not know. With only one year left before high school, I could honestly say that, so far, he was living his life with honor, fairness, kindness, and truth, and that had to make any mother proud. I hoped I wasn't missing something.

By the end of September, Andy suggested we take a trip, just the two of us, someplace safe and friendly, where we could begin to make new memories. Clearly, our relationship had been profoundly shaken.

Switzerland was my first choice, and Andy readily agreed. Playing travel agent, I packed our itinerary as full as a Swiss train schedule, beginning with a shopping spree at REI in downtown Seattle, where we outfitted ourselves with day packs, comfortable hiking boots and wool socks, first aid and water kits, compasses, headlamps, moleskin patches, and the latest lightweight hiking gear. We were set!

Leaving the children with their Nonny and Janelle, our babysitter, we answered the call to adventure.

Once in Zurich, we hopped on the train, stopping in various towns and villages that were nestled in valleys and surrounded by breathtaking views of the Alps. I'd visited Switzerland once before, when I was sixteen—Andy had been along, too. It was an organized camping trip through Europe for six weeks with three adults and twenty teenagers. Now, as an adult, I could fully appreciate the awesome beauty of the place.

Foregoing the cog rails, we hiked up and down the trails. One day, breathing hard on an especially steep trek, an old Swiss couple waved to us from their hut, exclaiming to their neighbors, "Look at those Americans. They're like slugs walking up the mountain." We hiked above the tree line, below the tree line, among the lush meadows. At the end of the day, blissfully tired and happy, we enjoyed velvety cheese fondue and German beer.

Switzerland, September 2006

On a side trip from Interlaken, we took the rail to the small town of Murren, a village that bowed to the Eiger, Jungfrau, and Monch. We had reservations at the Palace Hotel, built in the early 1900s when Switzerland was becoming a popular destination for tourists. Situated on a sunny plateau and encircled by steep cliffs, the Palace was highly recommended by all the travel books and websites. But, the peeling paint testified to grander times.

I counted six levels as we walked up the cobblestone road, noting the disco and laundry facilities on the basement level and the small dormer windows flung open in the attic. Bright red geraniums spilled from pots on either side of the entrance. Though the gardens were filled with color, they were in need of a gardener.

Sunlight streamed across the lobby, catching threadbare spots in the green floral carpet and revealing the hardwood floors below. Soaring upward was a grand staircase, etched with time and history. Every window framed a mountaintop. A warm and friendly staff greeted us, explaining apologetically that the hotel was under new ownership and due for renovation. Our room was at the end of the hall on the fourth floor. Once inside, I set my backpack on a chair by the window and breathed in the magnificent view. Murren felt like home.

Two days later, we checked out and left for an early morning rail to take us back down the steep mountain so we could travel on to Lausanne. Andy was some distance ahead when my hiking boot caught an edge and I stumbled, barely catching my balance before taking a nasty fall. Shaken, I pulled myself onto the embankment to catch my breath, watching the mountains emerge from a low layer of white, puffy clouds. Looking back toward the hotel, what I saw set my heart pounding. A teenage girl was perched Indian style in a far attic window overlooking the cliffs. She wore a green hooded sweatshirt and jeans. Her feet were bare. She waved at me, and I waved back. The September wind smacked my bare face.

At that moment, I understood that Sarah would be forever sixteen. I reached for the Canon hung around my neck, but if I took a photo, would the image appear? If I walked back, would she vanish from the window? I remembered Sarah rubbing my feet, promising she'd never leave me.

That moment was mine, so I said nothing to Andy. He was gradually relaxing as our adventure unfolded, the wrinkles of his rugged skin dissolving and the sadness in his eyes beginning to fade. He looked healthy and strong. Evoking sad memories would have been like riding the train back to a previous destination. But, I held it close to my heart.

Only now, as Andy and Caiti and Christopher read my story, does my family know of this sighting. I am now ready to share this moment with others.

On October 30, 2006, we moved into our new home. Warm, peaceful, comfortable, and filled with natural light, it had everything the cold rental house lacked. It was just right.

The day we moved in, I sensed that the end was near for Grandmom. Unpacking the boxes of china and crystal she had already passed on to me, I was filled with a strong sense of urgency. When I called to invite her to dinner, I reached her voicemail. Next day she returned the call, "It's Grandmom, honey. Listen. The way I feel today, I wouldn't feel strong enough to go. But maybe by Tuesday I'll be fine. Don't count on it, though. Don't make reservations just for me. If I'm well enough, I'd love to go. You're very sweet to invite me. Bye-bye."

I saved the message. Sometimes I replay it just to hear her voice.

The next morning, I abandoned the moving boxes and took the ferry over to visit her. Grandmom smiled as I knocked and entered her cheery, yellow room, with views of Mt. Rainier and Lake Washington, family photos on the windowsill. She was propped up in bed, hand extended as if I'd come to rescue her. For the first time, I felt no warmth in her hands. Her short white hair was matted to her head, showing bare spots on her scalp. Not a word of complaint came from her pale lips. But the pain was obvious. Under the white coverlet, she could barely move.

We spent the afternoon together. I helped her over to the small sofa, pulling our lunch from a brown paper bag, and holding her soup. She ate a few spoonsful. I opened the packaged Saltines. We laughed, recounting family stories and shared memories. There was the drive together, from Seattle to Portland, when I left for college, traveling in a blue 1979 Ford Mustang with a manual transmission, I driving and Grandmom in the passenger seat. My mouth was wadded with bubble gum, George Thorogood blaring from the speakers. We reminisced about Granddad, the shutterbug, who took his camera everywhere, producing stacks of out-of-focus, misaligned photos, and remembered years of Sunday night sports, eating Chinese take-out on TV trays in her den. She had the scoop on every player of our local Seahawks, Sonics, and Mariners, as well as every major player of the NFL, NBA, and MLB. She reminded me of our trip downtown in a long-ago February downpour to buy me a pair of pink saddle shoes I so desperately wanted when I was thirteen. Between memories, she ate the crackers.

Death does not wait for most people. But it seemed that Grandmom would have enough time to say her final goodbyes and leave this world with minimal suffering. I encouraged our family members to come quickly. Aunt Lindy caught a flight from Oakland the next day. Each of Grandmom's children arrived to spend time with her, filtering in and out of her apartment for the next three weeks. Her grandchildren made their final visits.

As her days dwindled, all seemed to be just as she intended. Her personal belongings were at a minimum: her black rosary—the beads worn by years of constant prayer, as she passed the rosary through her fingers, one bead and one set of Hail Mary's at a time, until the prayer of the rosary was completed each morning and night; her twin bed; a small carved wooden statue of the Madonna; the blue bag I'd knitted for her just before Sarah died; a picture of Granddad as a boy; a jar of Pond's hand cream; one tube of lipstick; two pairs of comfortable shoes, and several freshly pressed outfits. She said her last goodbyes. Her mind was clear, her words few but precise. Then, she rested in preparation for her passage.

Three days before Thanksgiving, my older brother Geordie arrived. Sometimes difficult to locate, Geordie lives a solitary life, exploring meditation, faith, and God. His only map, a compass of the heart.

For the next three days, he prayed with Grandmom, her rosary beads gripped tightly, telling me that he felt Sarah's presence in the room. With her guidance, he prayed in the words and spirit of Grandmom's Christian tradition, summoning the aid and comfort of Jesus Christ.

Finally at 6:00 a.m. on Thanksgiving Day 2007, Grandmom took her last breath, her lips forming a gentle smile, wrinkles becoming relaxed and smoothed, dissolving into the beauty of her youth, making her a beautiful young girl once again.

Raising himself from the cold metal chair beside her bed, Geordie laid Grandmom's arms across her chest, hands clasped together, resting over her heart, as in prayer. What a full and honorable life Grandmom had led, the kind of long and meaningful journey that everyone wishes for themselves and their children.

Before spending the next forty-nine days in prayer, Geordie told me of his belief that all paths of good intention would lead to Sarah's new Home. I have never argued with him on that point. He says the back door to Sarah's Home is always open for him.

The coroner's office removed Grandmom's body from her apartment in late morning as the turkey went into the oven. Yes, there was sadness that holiday, but we had so much to be thankful for.

Memories and happy stories of Grandmom filled that Thanksgiving holiday. I had to believe that she was with us, celebrating the continuation of family and traditions. A generation had passed, and the next generation had raised the torch to celebrate the future. Blessings were said. The turkey was carved. We explained to Annie and Mary that Great-grandmom would be with Sarah now—a second person to pray for each night, another angel watching over them.

spring, year three

> Our background and circumstances may have influenced
> who we are, but we are responsible for who we become.
> —Barbara Geraci

Thirty-two months had passed since Sarah's death, and now April hinted at a warm summer hidden under the crisp marine air. The rains took a hiatus. Swallows returned earlier than usual in a great swoop— hundreds of them dashing left, returning right. For us, spring begins with the return of the heron. We've named him Albert. Our shoreline is his home, where he mates and nests for the season. Perched on large rocks that protrude as the tide goes about its business, holding still, ready to spear swimming prey, Albert is like one of the eagles crowning the highest limbs of the hemlocks dotting the shoreline, though the eagles are with us year-round.

Albert

That Easter Sunday, as we gathered for our annual egg hunt, I hid the golden egg at the base of an old maple, with just a glimmer of gold hinting at the treasure. On any given day, competition runs deep in our family, and that day was no exception. The little ones race against the oldest, as the oldest scramble to keep up. Shouts of "I saw it first" are not entirely uncommon, even though it's just an egg and isn't real gold. But everyone places five dollars in the egg bucket, so the prize money is real.

Inside, Andy woke, unsteady on his feet, throbbing headache, his chest tight, limbs visibly twitching, palms of his hands clammy and cold. He greeted everyone as they arrived but quickly retreated to the bedroom and closed the door, lying in bed all day, limbs stretched out, windows flung open, hoping the fresh air would ease his nausea.

Later, after family and friends had gone and the children were asleep, the feelings Andy had locked inside for so long began to pour out in a torrent of anguish and tears, as though he had entered the church confessional to avow years of sins. He believed that if he and Christopher had flown home on Monday morning, as planned, Sarah would have slept in her own bed Sunday night and she would still be alive.

Before Sarah's accident, their relationship was gradually improving; yet, it was still strained. And, because the girls were not allowed to have friends over without prior permission, they often spent time with their friends' families rather than their own. But I knew there was no connection between Andy's early return and Sarah's death. She hadn't spent the night out because her stepdad was coming home; she just wanted to be with her friends. She was sixteen years old, and it was the end of summer. How difficult it must have been for Andy to finally open that heavy door of grief and regret that he had locked so firmly behind him.

Throughout the night until traces of light began to appear on the horizon, Andy poured out his long-buried guilt and disappointment in so many areas of his life, from teenage mishaps to the death of his parents to Sarah's accident. No wonder he had shut them away.

Until that night, I had not known if our marriage could survive. After that night, I knew it would. Sarah's death was not the only strain on our marriage, but it opened the door for a stronger and more loving family.

Change had arrived.

For Andy to stop and allow himself time to heal—body and soul— patience and compassion were essential. It was a personal battle that only he could win or lose. He had lived in a world of unattainable expectations, with a "should" around every corner. There were friends he should have—those arranged friendships assumed with his privileged birth. There were favors he should grant because he shouldn't say no. There was the work he should do, the financial successes he was expected to achieve, with no time left over to balance work with the people he loved and the things he loved to do. There were public events and donations that were not necessarily those he would have chosen for himself.

By mid-April, the daffodils and white tulips made way for calla lilies, ornamental grasses, blue hostas, and pink peony shoots. Warm, sunny days of late spring and summer rolled in. Andy paused, taking time alone when he needed space around him, time alone with me, and time to know our children better. He visited with Father Quigg, seeking answers and friendship, further exploring the Catholic traditions. His spiritual journey led to a conversion to Catholicism in December 2008. I'd like to think that Sarah helped him on his path.

Andy cut back on his workload in Seattle, pursued a long-held interest in yoga, and began studying art. He swam and walked daily and had sessions with the same therapist I had seen in Seattle. Through the persistence and integrity he applied to all this effort, his life opened to new possibilities.

Caiti and Annie, spring 2007

Caiti finished her first year of college in May 2007, at last, a year that produced more ups than downs for her. Overcoming her fears, she had blossomed in a new setting with new faces. New friends, new studies, a new life filled the voids. She shared herself and her story in her own way and in her own time. She joined a sorority, enjoyed social events, and immersed herself in her studies—mostly business and political science. Gradually, Caiti began to know and accept herself as one, instead of two. To see her smiling again was the greatest gift of all. I never tire of that smile.

summer, year three

This will surprise you. When the civil lawsuits were finally settled, our family received a proportional award. The fact that our daughter had died had no greater consequence than the circumstances of the other kids who were injured. I sat in the mediation room listening to a variety of lawyers as they droned on about the statistical value of death, injury, umbrella policies, insurance proceeds, and attorney fees. Somehow, I had harbored the illusion that I would feel better—more

at peace, more whole—when the legal procedures were said and done.
I was wrong.

> *When one door of happiness closes, another opens;*
> *But we often look so long at the closed door that*
> *We do not see the one that has opened for us.*
>
> —Helen Keller

And how about me? In those three years after Sarah's accident, attempts to venture outside my emotional shell had failed. I was comfortable only in intimate settings or away from home where nobody knew our story, where no rehashing or explanations were necessary. I didn't want to feel compelled to defend myself, make excuses for Sarah, or lie about how we were doing. Once in a while, I accepted invitations to parties or coffee with a friend, only to cancel at the last minute. But finally, finally, during that third August, something changed.

I donned a pink sundress and straw hat and forced myself to attend the annual garden party at the Bloedel Reserve, a garden retreat on the north end of Bainbridge where walking trails meander through groves of ferns and patches of moss, across open meadows, around small lakes, a reflection pond, and a man-made waterfall, and then past the Japanese Tea House, ending at the French Chateau where Prentice and Virginia Bloedel had raised a family in the mid-1900s. The Bloedels had been friends of Andy's parents, so when I entered the dining room, I imagined the four adults gathered around the English dining table, sharing an elegant dinner of French wine and wild duck. Thinking of that friendship and the lovely, candlelit dinners in this beautiful room, I was reminded of many valued friendships that had gone away. Admiring Caiti's efforts to establish herself at college, make new friends, and become more comfortable with herself, I resolved to follow her example.

Not as confident as my husband in social settings, I mingled with a few guests, knowing if I grew uncomfortable, I could escape to the shady trails. Suddenly, something felt different. Catching my reflection in the mirror in that old dining room, I saw myself smiling.

 *year four*

When terrible tragedy strikes your family, you see the sun outside, but inside, every day is dark and frightening. The time drags by, moment-by-moment, hour-by-hour, until one day ends and the next begins, like patterns of concentric circles. But eventually, as the sun continues to rise and set, life returns. It's not the same. It will never be the same. But, nonetheless, it is a gift.

fall and winter, year four

Annie began preschool two weeks after Sarah's third anniversary. On her first day of school, when asked about her family, she said there were five children and she was the littlest. She called Sarah the sister who lived in her heart, who'd been killed in a car crash, who was her angel, the first star to shine each night.

Each picture Annie drew included Sarah. Some pictures showed Sarah and Annie picking flowers or sitting together in a boat on the water or walking hand in hand. In some pictures, Sarah appeared in the clouds above, with Annie below, head pointed upward. The sky was always blue.

Her remarks and questions continue to be spontaneous and random. Is Sarah with baby Jesus? Did Sarah say, "Hi," to Great-grandmom when she got to Heaven? Do they live together now? Will Lady be with Sarah when she dies? Why can't I see Sarah now? What do angels look like? Do they fly like birds? Then there are the questions that make me think: Does it hurt to die? Why do some people die when they're old and some when they're young? How do you get from here to heaven? When I die, will I be a ghost or an angel? How does Sarah live in my heart? Does Sarah still look like Caiti? Are they still twins? I am always caught off-guard.

When Caiti and Sarah were little, they were always together, sharing the same bedroom, having the same teachers, joining the same activities, hanging out with the same friends. Sarah led the way while Caiti followed. Both were strong but in complementary ways. They depended on each other: two halves striving to be a whole. I never considered the importance of twins being separate individuals. If I could have foreseen the tragedy we were living out, I'd never have encouraged their lives melding together so much. Caiti and Sarah had never been their own persons in that shared lifetime.

I wanted to put that insight to work with Annie and Mary, now ages three and four. I determined, right then and there, that each would know her own strengths and weaknesses and be encouraged to claim her individuality. Each girl would have her own friends, her own spaces, and her own ideas. Each would be independent, capable, and whole. This was one of those generous second chances.

After Sarah's accident, my dog died, then my grandparents died. Somehow, this overwhelming tidal wave of loss opened up a crisis of shame, guilt, and regret buried deep in my psyche. Losing Sarah opened vulnerability in me that, like Andy, I had locked away. Suddenly, my inner turmoil spotlighted those conflicts, exposing them like open wounds.

What surprised me most was that the turmoil became a catalyst to resolving these conflicts. Each death drew me closer to my feelings, my hopes, my faith—who I was as a mother, as a wife, as a friend—what gave meaning to my life. Rather than confining myself to loss and grief, the deaths in my family have made me more aware of how truly precious life is. Each death has ultimately validated the beauty of living.

spring and summer, year four

In the spring of 2008, as the apple trees sprang forth with soft, white blossoms, our family was breathing again. We were enjoying the new house. We were returning to family activities that, once, had evoked too many sad memories.

For Caiti, time had softened the edges of her painful memories and preserved the ones that brought joy. In spreading her wings, she began to believe in herself, not again, but for the first time. Maybe that was Sarah's greatest gift to her sister. Dreaming of a large existence, of living purposeful lives and making a contribution—that was what my twins had talked about as they lay in bed at night. Now, Caiti would carry on for both of them.

Caiti decided to finish college at the University of Washington. Moving back to Seattle at the end of her sophomore year, she met a young man, Shaun, with whom she liked to spend time. I worried that she might get hurt. I doubted if anyone could understand the emotional scarring Caiti carried, if someone who had never suffered such losses could understand someone who had. But, Caiti had come into her own, living strong and making her own decisions.

From the start, Shaun was a kindred spirit, holding Caiti's fragile heart delicately with truth, kindness, and love. I imagined that Sarah approved.

Christopher seemed stable and content. Through his middle school years, we'd purposely sheltered him somewhat from painful memories of Sarah's accident. The community at Hyla Middle School, always sensitive to our family's situation, encouraged Christopher to let down his guard and accept life with all its ups and downs. He switched from soccer to lacrosse, performed in Shakespeare's *As You Like It*, surfed the Oregon Coast with his teachers, added to his cooking skills, and learned to knit. Hyla grounded him in the importance of today and the pleasure of simplicity—fostering and nurturing his acceptance of life's uncertainties. Again, I was proud to be Christopher's mother. He was ready now for high school. I imagined Sarah would agree.

My life also began a gentle transformation. The garden party at the Bloedel Reserve was a timid beginning, followed by a disheartening setback. Once again, my sleeping habits disintegrated. I struggled for confidence and couldn't seem to focus. I tried supplements and nutrition, yoga and trail running, self-help books, talk therapy, biofeedback for posttraumatic stress disorder, and overnight sleep studies at Harborview Medical Center in Seattle. Nothing helped.

Never far from my consciousness was the grief and guilt. If I hadn't caved to Sarah's nagging request to spend the night at a friend's house, she would have been in her own bed. If she hadn't left her friend's house that Sunday night and stayed where she was supposed to be, she would still be home today.

I couldn't seem to stop the cycle of fear and worry, staying awake at night until my children were home, waiting anxiously after school to hear them come in the door. Once everyone was safe at home, I could breathe and let go of my vigilance until the next day when it started again.

It would take a potluck dinner to give me the courage to fully live and love again. We are fortunate to have local, sustainable farms that grow beautiful organic vegetables and fruits on the island. Every Tuesday, throughout that spring and summer, we took home, and greatly enjoyed, our colorful assortment from the farmers. When the growing season peaked in mid-August, they invited us to a potluck.

About thirteen families attended, each placing a favorite vegetarian dish on the long wooden table covered by a sun-yellow cloth. (I baked two apple pies.) Even our children were intrigued by the variety and aroma of the spread.

Before sharing the meal, the three young farmers—college graduates, mid-twenties—walked us through areas of the twenty acres, inviting us to pick strawberries or carrots as they explained the farming system.

They showed us the catchall used for irrigating with rainwater. Annie picked a handful of the sweet red berries.

After the tour, we joined around the picnic table and said a simple grace, acknowledging the bounty before us. The girls and I sat on boulders, off to the side, while Andy settled into conversation with one of the owners, a woman with long, luxuriant silver hair, a lovely face, and a nurturing presence. I'd not met her before.

Andy asked quietly, "How are you doing?"

She said, "It's been a living nightmare." She wasn't afraid of the truth.

I knew that her middle son, several years older than Caiti and Sarah, had been in a motorcycle accident. Though he survived, he was paralyzed for life, requiring constant care. My eyes settled on her son, sitting quietly in his wheelchair at the far end of the table. Listening to this wise and compassionate mother, I felt Sarah's presence.

In that open field with the midday sun bearing down, my mind began to race. Thoughts I'd never had. Thoughts I'd been too afraid to think. Or maybe I'd just never allowed myself those thoughts.

What if Sarah had survived her accident only to be paralyzed for the rest of her life? What if she had to suffer through years of disability and illness? What if she suffered terrible pain? I had such respect for these parents and their son.

Though I never got to say goodbye to Sarah, I would never have to see the helplessness in her eyes. Would the grieving process have been more bearable if death was expected, if I'd had the chance to say goodbye? If death had to come, what was the greater blessing? To live and suffer? To suffer and die? Or, to die without suffering?

I wanted to believe that Sarah was given a choice—that she left sooner, rather than later, because she understood the journey that lay ahead. I wanted to believe she heard Caiti's giggle, laughed with me, and slapped her brother a high-five. No time for goodbyes. I wanted to believe that she thought of us in those final moments.

I wanted to believe my grandfather, Papa, opened his loving arms to greet Sarah at death's door, with peace ringing in his voice, removing all pain from the accident, while a brilliant Light healed her wounds and illuminated her soft blue eyes and beckoning smile. I wanted to believe Papa, in his reasonableness, knew what was best for Sarah, and that she trusted in him. I hoped that she would remember when Papa had given her a gold coin and a bright, purple Schwinn bicycle to celebrate her fourth birthday.

I wanted to believe Sarah was present when the two strangers knocked at our door to tell us that she had been killed, that she filled me with warmth as I was gasping for air, stunned with grief, and locked in prayer. I have to believe that Sarah will never leave us.

The afternoon of the potluck, I questioned the Angel of Death for the last time. Death happens. Accidents happen. People face tragedy as best they can. I could never know more than that. I can accept that life isn't fair, that bad things happen, that Mother Nature continues of her own accord, without explanation. I don't know if everything is God's will. And I don't hold God responsible for taking Sarah from us. I believe in a God who helps me, not a God who punishes me. And I believe He will never abandon me.

Perhaps, someday, I'll be able to thank that mother for sharing her story and changing my life. Often it is the simplest things, the simplest statements, which change our lives.

After the potluck, I made two important promises to myself.

First: When life isn't good, let truth lead the way. I don't need to hide or be ashamed of my feelings. Life needs to be authentic.

Second: Never again would I claim only four children. I had five children, and one of them died. A beautiful child once lived in my home. Now, she lives in my heart. I can still smile and live a joyful life.

We cannot cure the world of sorrows,
But we can choose to live in joy.
—Joseph Campbell

 # *august* 23, 2009

The highest tribute to the dead is not grief but gratitude.
—Thornton Wilder

Today, as with each August 23, I envision Sarah perched atop the worn granite tombstone marked L'Abbe. I picture her watching us as we gather to share our annual picnic in this calm and serene place.

Yesterday, in the early evening hours, Caiti visited Sarah's grave, preparing herself for this annual memorial. As the glow of the sun faded west over the Olympics and bounced off the ripples of Lake Washington, Caiti and Shaun circled the cemetery on foot, appreciating the new flowers, taking a deep breath when strolling past a glossy, new nameplate. Caiti was at peace. Comfortably, they settled next to Sarah's headstone. No words spoken. Few tears.

Before leaving for Calvary this morning, I finally feel strong enough to drive down Tolo Road. It has been five long years. I touch the wooden cross with both hands and tie a yellow helium balloon with a smiley face to the horizontal timber. A ceramic angel sits atop the post guarding a small weather-beaten teddy bear. Still scattered under ferns and bramble are remnants from the accident. Standing there, I wonder if Sarah misses me as much as I miss her.

As I attach the balloon, my ears strain to hear a distant voice. "Enough is enough. Five years. You guys have shed enough tears to drown yourselves. I've seen your anger towards those involved and towards me. The resentments are harsh. They hurt. Please accept my death. I've given gifts no one can ever take from you. Those gifts are the reason for my living here with you, and they're the reason for my living beyond your grasp. Take them. That way, you'll honor my life. It'll be complete. Then I can journey on." I realize I've been holding Sarah with my grief. Tears stream down my cheeks. Today, I know we must let her go.

Five years have passed. That is about a third of Sarah's lifetime. Including Sarah, four kids from her kindergarten class are now dead. One committed suicide. Two were killed in car crashes. One died from cancer. Four kids out of nineteen, that's more than twenty percent of her kindergarten class. Tragedies touch many families. Sarah would be twenty-one this year. How can I not look at the children in Annie's kindergarten class and wonder who will live and who will die before their twenty-first birthday?

Sarah's last year here with us was good. She was able to put *fun* into living without interrupting anyone's life. Being a teenager today isn't easy, especially confined to an island. Teenagers stress themselves out constantly, usually unintentionally, always unnecessary. Most parents expect too much of that age group. The peer pressure from those in teen circles and those outside can be devastating, too obsessive for most kids. And I think it's fair to say most never look at their own mortality. Never in a million years can I imagine Sarah looked at hers. For Sarah, life was here and now and ready to be lived. I cannot deny that Sarah sometimes had little regard for life. And I felt betrayed as a mother. Not as if I'd been a bad parent, but as if my words had been strangled. Life is a learning experience. And maybe, subconsciously, Sarah did realize her life would end sooner than most people she hung with.

I know now that time heals if time is allowed. If you allow yourself to feel the dark depths of pain, returning there without fear—and it will return, sometimes when you least expect it—and you can weave that profound pain into your life, then death doesn't sink too far into your bones. If you can't allow your heart to mend, death takes you. Accepting the loss of a loved one is to release, but not erase. To hold. But not to hold the pain.

Today, we've agreed to set Sarah free. We accept her death. I know she's shared the pain gripping our hearts these five years. And I know she's shared in the love that has grown within each of us. We have found her gifts. We are ready to release her and allow her to journey on.

Keeping with tradition, Papa Ed has cleared the dead flowers and prepared the area for this day's celebration of Sarah's life. The pink geraniums explode with color. A little shade from the Prairiefire tree, now reaching sixteen feet above us, remarks on the passage of time, its blossoms long gone by late summer.

I watch my husband at the gravesite, completely present, his arms around Caiti and Christopher, walking toward me. His every movement details devotion to his family. Alert. Compassionate. Attentive. Each guest receives a solid hug. He offers his left arm to Father Quigg, tucking the worn leather-bound Bible under his right arm, holy water in his right hand for the blessing. We recite a few prayers and tell another story. Songs are sung. Tears are shed, though without the bitterness of earlier years.

This year, for the first time, Mary and Annie join the anniversary picnic. I hear Annie ask Mary, "Is Sarah really below my feet?" Mary tells her not to ask such questions. I am certain my youngest girls are ready to decipher love and grief. Annie brings a clear helium balloon with a small pink pig rattling inside.

Earlier in the week, she has asked to take a gift to the cemetery, hoping that her balloon will reach Sarah in heaven. Standing in the center of the circle, she unclenches her fist from the pink string and sends the balloon drifting upward. The skies are clear. We all stand—transfixed—until it disappears into the ethers. Annie blows kisses. We sing "Amazing Grace."

As I am packing up the leftovers, the cemetery manager stops to say hello. I hand him a plate of lunch. He radios three maintenance men who finish up the sandwiches, fruit, chips, and peanut butter cookies.

They offer the girls a ride in their tractor. Stories of Sarah's burial and anniversaries are shared. They remember the events. One maintenance man, Ed, has worked at Calvary for thirty-five years.

While the bees feast on watermelon rinds, I imagine Sarah waving goodbye as we return to our cars.

Calvary now feels like home: intimate ... warm ... people who care. It feels as if the living embrace the dead, as if Sarah's death brings a closeness and joy to all of us.

Caiti returns to her apartment and opens the book Sarah gave her in sixth grade. She reads the words on the last page: "Keep this book forever for I will be with you long after I die. Take good care of it, Caiti, my sister, my twin."

I go home and flip through the guest book from Sarah's memorial celebration: 627 signatures. What an honor to have shared that afternoon in August 2004 with so many who were there for us.

I look through the journal left at the crash site. The bold words written by a friend—or maybe a stranger—on the first page of the journal are so true: "Learn 2 Live, Live 2 Love." After Sarah died, I had misinterpreted the phrase thinking it was "Live 2 Love, Love 2 Live." One thousand green wristbands were distributed island-wide with that misconstrued phase. Now that life is over, I know for certain that Sarah lived her sixteen years by both mottos. I understand my daughter better than I thought.

I pull Sarah's autobiography from her trunk, reading again the words at the end of her essay: "And now it is time for my story to end, because we have finally reached the beginning."

epilogue 2011

Life signifies everything it ever has; the thread is not cut.
Why would I be out of your thoughts
Just because I'm out of your sight?
I am not far, just on the other side of the path.

—St. Augustine

annie

Annie has similarities to Sarah. Small things: a twist of the nose, the furrowing of eyebrows, her stride that says, "Watch out, here I come," and of course, the familiar humor. Perhaps as simple as shared genetic traits, these happy reminders lessen the tears that sometimes come for no reason at all, or bring an unexpected smile. Annie is seven, going on eight. But she seems like Sarah, twenty-three going on twenty-four. Or maybe Sarah is forever sixteen.

Annie enjoys drawing and pottery, reading and writing stories, singing and the theater. This past summer she played an Oompa-Loompa in *Willie Wonka and the Chocolate Factory*. Andy has promised to teach her to surf and fly fish. Each night, her prayers include Sarah and her great-grandmom; her friends, classmates, and teachers; peace in the world; hungry, cold children; mothers and fathers; and love. And she gives thanks for her blessings, including her health.

One recent morning, flipping through the newspaper, I spot a full-page ad about a DVD-release of *Gone with the Wind*. Annie glances at the page and exclaims, "Oh, that's Rhett Butler and Scarlett O'Hara."

I pause, tweaking my neck. Annie, exposed only once to this movie, was six months old at the time. I smile to myself. Maybe this is one of those moments Sarah takes to say, "Hey, I am still here."

mary

Like the Energizer Bunny, Mary is full of get-up-and-go. She wakes with a smile, smiles all day, and goes to sleep smiling. Nothing seems to rattle her. And when it does, she shakes it off easily, without commotion. I envy her resilience.

Naturally athletic like her father, Mary loves everything out-of-doors: running around the track, hiking, swimming, and biking. Christopher coaches her soccer team. Her dad takes her to Snoqualmie Pass in the winter so she can compete on the ski team. She loves school, reading, and writing stories. Dogs are her favorite animals. She plans to volunteer at the Westsound Wildlife Shelter when she is a teenager.

When Mary was a baby, Sarah would cradle her in both arms like a football, remarking that Mary's whole world had just begun, that she had a whole life to live and explore. Sarah seemed blown away by that thought. Mary's birth seemed to ease Sarah away from her turmoil, toward the love she embraced during her final year. Perhaps the cuddling and giggles shared between teenager and baby have contributed to Mary's particular joy for life.

For Mary and Annie, Sarah is known only through borrowed memories gleaned from the stories and photos we share with them. They can never experience her personality or the sound of her laugh. They ask questions, and our answers shape ideas in their minds. Each filters pieces to keep, letting go of the rest. Never expecting Sarah to walk through the front door or needing to grieve for her, they knew only the pain and confusion that had washed over our family. But when asked about their family, they reply, "I have three sisters and one brother." They understand that their mother has five children, all treasured and equally important.

Mary's and Annie's giggles and smiles and daily needs kept our family afloat during the darkest times. I'll be forever grateful to them for their boundless resilience and energy.

christopher

Christopher was ten when Sarah was killed. Now he's older than Sarah will ever be. He worked fulltime this summer in a chowder house, commuting on the ferry to Seattle. Now that school has started, he works with a local caterer some weekends. As a senior in high school, his academic strengths are in science and math. Surfing, lacrosse, snowboarding, woodworking, experiments, and inventing are his passions. The fire cadet program, sports and crossfit, friends, and coaching Mary's soccer team also fill his time. He chooses Mary Oliver's quote—*Tell me, what do you plan to do with your one wild and precious life?*—to caption his senior photo in the yearbook. On occasion, high school temptations have captured his better judgment. On his eighteenth birthday, he had Sarah's tattoo inked in black and white on his right rib cage, about six inches tall with wings and a halo. I am appalled at the size, but he loves it.

Christopher's tattoo

Christopher fully understands the toll taken by Sarah's death, not just for him but for me, our family, and Sarah's friends. He has learned that, even as families survive tragedy, the effects continue to ripple outward far into the future. He knows firsthand that personal choices come with consequences, and he understands that our lives are intertwined, like yarns of the chunky wool hats he's knitted. How easily it can all unravel! Maturity comes with time. I am certain Sarah's gifts will sustain him.

caiti

Caiti graduated from the University of Washington in the summer of 2010, and began work at Microsoft that fall. Focused on applying to business school, she studies for the GMAT's and takes global business and language classes in the evening. Notebooks of scribbled fashion designs may predict her future. One day, perhaps, she'll combine her business background with her interest in fashion and open her own boutique.

August 2010

Caiti is loyal in her relationships, giving them priority in her life. She visits the cemetery, sometimes alone, sometimes with Shaun. When Sarah was alive, they had a world of their own. Now Caiti has expanded the map of her life.

The cord between Caiti and me has gently slipped away, strand by strand, in a transformation from parent-child to a rich and rewarding mother-daughter friendship.

We have good times together. We've done Las Vegas, taken in many chick flicks, shopped, done the spa thing, and had dinner atop the Space Needle. She's much prettier now than when the twins were sixteen. And she'll tell you that. But I like to imagine that they still look the same. When I look at Caiti, I will always see Sarah, too.

She and Christopher share good times—dinners and movies and hanging out in his room, talking late into the night. He stays at her apartment and spends time with her boyfriend. They're Facebook friends. For each of his birthdays and Christmas, Caiti buys the perfect present for him.

Recently when we moved Caiti from one apartment to another, I lifted the box spring mattress, readying it for the U-Haul truck, and found a blue box. A large note attached read, "DO NOT STEAL. To anyone thinking of taking this fireproof safe: There is nothing of value to you in here. These are keepsakes from my twin sister who died. These are my most special things—please, please do not take. Take anything but this." Caiti's contact info was written clearly on the lid, in case the box was stolen and left for trash. I put the small box on the passenger seat of her car instead of loading it into the U-Haul.

When she marries, I know she'll ask Sarah to be her maid-of-honor, inviting her shimmering witness in the candlelight, as Caiti claims a full and joyous life.

andy

Andy and I share morning coffee; his black, mine with a hint of cream. Scanning the water's surface for signs of salmon jumping, we say hello to the herons, perched on rock formations protruding through the tidal flow, as they wait for breakfast to swim past. The school bus comes for the girls at 7:15. Then, Andy begins his workday. Some days he works from home, sharing lunch with me; other days he takes the ferry into Seattle.

Paddle boarding has become his new passion. Islanders see him coming from miles away, balanced to catch the waves, hugging the shoreline. Yoga, hiking, masters swimming, and biking on the trainer in our family room fill the rainy days. When the ski season opens, he's there for first tracks, fluid and graceful as he sails through the powder. Just as elegant to watch is the cast of his fly rod, a perfect loop landing the dry fly on a pocket of fish ready to gulp.

We speak infrequently of Sarah's accident, but Andy is comfortable saying her name and sharing the good memories. He doesn't light Sarah's candle in the kitchen window, but he sometimes browses through the family photo albums. Often, he likes to sit and take everything in, balanced in the moment—healthy, fit, calm, and rested.

and me

My family is surviving and thriving. Each lives with Sarah's gifts, each honoring her life. Love has strengthened us in ways far beyond my expectations. I am proud of us and respect what we have endured.

It was twenty-one years from the birth of my twins to the day my last child caught the school bus for kindergarten. I will be fifty-eight when that last child leaves for college. Now that all the kids are in school, I enjoy morning walks with Lady. The trails are wide open through old-growth Douglas firs, past young maples and alders. My thoughts ramble. I imagine Sarah and Emmett joining us, making a foursome, the dogs content to wander at their own pace without a leash. I speak out loud to Sarah as we make our way on the trail. She responds with the sudden rush of a blue jay landing on a nearby branch or a tree swaying in the wind or a ray of sunshine splashing on a large maple leaf.

As days drift by, the fall leaves burst into shades of brilliant reds, oranges, and yellows. Then the bare limbs stand naked, the leaves fallen away, a carpet to nourish the earth. When winter arrives, the rains bear that pungent smell of rich, decomposing soil. I imagine Sarah following my footprints along the damp paths, walking delicately, not disturbing a twig or crushing a leaf. Sometimes I imagine following her footprints.

Things have become less complicated. Now I can think while I grocery shop, no child in tow begging for something sweet. I grab a take-out lunch of soup or sushi and sit in the car in some remote parking space, Sarah's photo still taped to the corner of my windshield. I often reflect on her.

Time has slowed. I have bought the two adjacent cemetery plots next to Sarah's grave. My reasoning is simple: I want my family to be together. It could be a midlife crisis. Certainly, nobody I know is buying cemetery plots in her forties. For me, it's preparing for the obvious. Christopher would tell you it's just his mother leaving nothing to chance, being too responsible.

Every February 5, to mark Sarah's birthday, I arrive at Calvary with a bouquet of pink Gerbera daisies, utter a prayer or two, and engage in a moment of silence and a few tears. I note that others have also been to the cemetery that day. I'm sure Sarah knows she has not been forgotten. For the rest of the day, we honor Caiti, as she celebrates her birthday.

Each night, before I prepare the family dinner, I light Sarah's candle. The votive glows against those tropical tans and healthy faces in the photo. I still recall the beautiful scent of the plumeria leis. The glowing light represents something different to each of us. For me, I know my daughter is present at our table. I'd like to believe that Andy feels the same. Maybe for Caiti and Christopher, the candlelight represents hope. And, perhaps for them, too, it keeps Sarah's memory alive. I am not certain, and I have not asked. Death is personal. Yes, death is very personal.

Lighting a special candle is as much a part of my nightly routine as reciting bedtime prayers. I linger in the kitchen, enjoying the final cleanup of the night, while the quiet returns to our home. The candle burns well into the night, after the kitchen lights are turned off for the evening and the children are safely tucked in their beds. When it flickers out, I know all is well and I can sleep.

I am free from the agony of asking why. I've learned to accept that death is a part of life. Both, constants. I don't believe Sarah's death was difficult or painful for her. I think of it as a few seconds. And life ended. Like so many, I believed that tragedies happened somewhere else, to other families, and were something we only read about. Surely, it couldn't touch us, certainly not one of our children. I believed that death came after a life had been fully lived, when one was long past childhood. I was wrong. Death comes when it will.

I don't believe it's important where or how Sarah has spent these last years or what her new world is all about. Those details have no importance to me beyond my belief that warmth and Light and love mercifully fill the void. What matters in my heart is knowing that Sarah didn't disappear when she left this world. I find her all around me, sometimes in the kindness of a friend, or even strangers. I've come to know her presence, the touch of her fingertips, her smell and her warmth.

I believe she'll continue to visit. She comes when we least expect her, making herself known with little clues—handprints, perhaps, or lost keys, some minor electrical or technical mishap, or sudden echoes of scent or sound. She'll see me smile or hear my laugh, and she'll know we've connected. She made a promise that she would never leave us, and Sarah never breaks a promise.

Unlike my grandparents who lived many years, visitations from them weren't necessary for their journeys into the world beyond ours. Accepting their death wasn't a critical factor in our grief. Their lives were no more complete than Sarah's, but they'd lived many years, leaving us with much love and many memories to cherish.

I don't believe in coincidences anymore or in the limitations of our five senses. There is purpose shining through everything, an implicit order to the universe. I am convinced that right now in this moment, we are all in the place where we are meant to be.

As Sarah's life and death have unfolded, I have learned gratitude for the small, everyday joys, the gifts that only appreciating the here and now can bring. I understand that learning to live and love is a lifelong process and that our greatest gift is today. But I've also come to know that love defines my journey, going deeper than the here and now, beyond my physical being. Love surrounds me—defining who I am and what I will leave behind. I am convinced that nothing else matters when the end comes.

But just as important, I know for sure that I never walk alone.